Enjoy the Good News

Enjoy the Good News

A New Testament guide

Alan Hogan

ATF Theology
Adelaide
2016

Published in Australia by ATF Press 2016
© The author claims copyright. All rights reserved.
Content may be freely copied, but only if for individual or group study or educational purposes. Otherwise, subject to the Copyright Act 1968 (Cth), no part may be copied or reproduced without written permission from the author.

National Library of Australia Cataloguing-in-Publication entry

Creator: Hogan, A. E. (Alan Eugene) author.

Title: Enjoy the Good News : a New Testament guide / Alan Hogan Llb MA.

ISBN:
978-1-925232-85-1 Paperback
978-1-925232-86-8 Hardback
978-1-925232-87-5 ePub
978-1-925232-88-2 Kindle
978-1-925232-89-9 PDF

Subjects: Bible. New Testament.
Bible. New Testament--Commentaries.
Bible. New Testament--Criticism, interpretation, etc.

Dewey Number: 225.7

Cover design and Layout/Artwork by Astrid Sengkey
Text Minion Pro Size 10 &11
Published by:

www.atfpress.com

An imprint of the ATF Ltd.
PO Box 504
Hindmarsh, SA 5007
ABN 90 116 359 963
www.atfpress.com
Making a lasting impact

Contents

Foreword		vii
Preface		xi
Introduction — How to use this book		xvii
Part 1 Origins of the New Testament		**1**
Chapter 1	The times, the places, the people	3
Chapter 2	The manuscript evidence	15
Chapter 3	The evolution of the canon	25
Part 2 Reading the New Testament		**29**
Chapter 4	The Acts of the Apostles	31
Chapter 5	The letters of Paul	37
Chapter 6	1 Thessalonians	41
Chapter 7	Galatians	45
Chapter 8	Philippians and Philemon	51
Chapter 9	1 Corinthians	55
Chapter 10	2 Corinthians5	61
Chapter 11	Romans	65
Chapter 12	Paul's attitude to women	71
Chapter 13	1 Peter	75
Chapter 14	How to read a gospel	77
Chapter 15	Gospel of Mark	83
Chapter 16	2 Thessalonians	91
Chapter 17	Colossians	93

Chapter 18	Ephesians	97
Chapter 19	Gospel according to Matthew	101
Chapter 20	Hebrews	115
Chapter 21	James	123
Chapter 22	Titus, 1 Timothy, 2 Timothy	127
Chapter 23	Luke Vol I—the Gospel	135
Chapter 24	Luke Vol II—Acts of the Apostles	153
Chapter 25	Jude and 2 Peter	173
Chapter 26	Book of Revelation	177
Chapter 27	Johannine literature	183
Chapter 28	The letters of John	187
Chapter 29	Gospel of John	191
Further reading		209
Image credits		211
Index		213

Foreword

It is with great pleasure that I write this Foreword to Alan Hogan's book *Enjoy the Good News: A New Testament guide.*

I had the privilege of teaching Alan as he embarked on his retirement project of studying for an MA (Biblical Studies) at Catholic Institute of Sydney. As a mature student, armed with the wisdom of life as well as his academic studies and years of work in the legal profession, Alan threw himself wholeheartedly into Biblical Studies at which he excelled.

Alan has now done what every theological graduate should be able to do: he has committed himself to write an Introduction to the New Testament, in which he presents in a concise manner, a clear understanding of these foundational writings of Christian life.

I recommend Alan's book to the audience for whom he has written: people who long to know more about the Scriptures, but who do not know where to begin or how to proceed. You will find in this introduction to the New Testament a most judicious balance of clearly explained technical details and an invitation to read the New Testament with confidence, in order to know Jesus our Messiah better and to live your Christian life more fully.

Alan makes it clear that he relies on the scholarly research of eminent Catholic biblical scholars both from Australia and overseas. Alan knows that we all like to have some sense of the background of a book of the New Testament when we set out to read it. Yet he also knows that these writings were composed and have been handed down in the Christian community not primarily to tell us details about the way in which they were written, but to enable us to know Jesus our Risen Lord and to strengthen us in living our Christian faith.

For each New Testament book or collection of books, Alan has written, with admirable brevity and clarity, a brief account of what the best of Catholic scholarship can offer us about the authorship and the originally intended audience of these writings. He writes clearly in a style that is easy to read yet conveys necessary historical, literary and theological information or interpretation. Alan makes it possible to see that each of these books is written to express faith in Jesus as it was developing in the rapidly growing and changing young Christian communities of the first century CE. Understanding something of the needs of these original faith communities helps us to grasp what these writings say to our own communities of faith today. Alan's book constantly keeps this question of the connection of the New Testament faith to our own, before his readers' eyes.

Alan has structured his own writing in a thoughtful way. He begins with some sound advice about how to use his book, which he intends as a companion to prayerful reading of the New Testament. He then writes a brief but succinct response to the historical questions most people have when they come to read the New Testament. These pages provide enough information, from reliable scholarship, to enable anyone to go on to read the New Testament with secure understanding.

Alan leads into the New Testament by summarising briefly the content of the Acts of the Apostles. Because the last two-thirds of Acts of the Apostles is about the apostle Paul, Alan's approach here is a sensible and very useful way to lead into a reading of the Letters of St Paul, the earliest written documents of the New Testament. Alan then treats the other New Testament writings in the chronological order in which they were written, insofar as the best scholarship is able to say. Reading the New Testament in this sequence helps to develop a sense of the organic emergence of the New Testament as the first generations of Christians began to live and understand a new faith.

For each book, Alan explains the shape or structure of the work, from beginning to end, so that it is easy to understand where a particular passage fits into the overall message the book conveys. He then reads through each work, summarising what it tells us in each section. You will find that reading Alan's survey of each book will help you to read the New Testament with confidence that you know what it is about. At the end of each major section Alan offers simple questions for reflection or for group sharing. Responding to these prompts to thought and conversation will enable the reader of Alan's book to express his or her own grasp of what the New Testament speaks to us. As we find words for what we have heard, we allow the Word of God to come alive in us.

It is for this purpose that Alan Hogan has written *Enjoy the Good News;* I commend it warmly to any Christian seeking to know Jesus better through the pages of the New Testament.

Dr Michele A. Connolly, rsj
Academic Dean
Lecturer in Biblical Studies
Catholic Institute of Sydney

Preface

The structure and purpose of this book are not original. They are taken from a book called *Enjoying the New Testament* by Margaret T Monro, first published by Longmans Green and Co in 1945.

It provided a plan for reading the whole of the New Testament, as far as possible in whole books, and mainly in the order in which they were written. Its purpose was to provide easier access to the text itself. It contained therefore, not a verse by verse commentary on the New Testament books, but such information and background to each work as would enable its readers to understand when, why and in what circumstances it was written, and what message the author intended to convey.

It was expressly not a work of scholarship, but in Margaret Monro's own words, 'a springboard for a dive into the living waters of God's Word.'

When I eventually read and used her book, and then used it together with a group of friends to experience the whole of the New Testament, my understanding and love of the Scriptures was greatly enhanced. (In my retirement from life as a lawyer I was even moved to undertake further formal study of them.) Others, I thought, might profit from a similar experience.

But not only is her book long out of print, a lot has happened in New Testament scholarship since 1945. When Margaret Monro wrote, the church had only recently begun to recover from its long reaction to Protestantism, Rationalism and Modernism. As she expressed it, 'While these issues were being thrashed out, the laity had to stand aside, and that in their own interests. Now, however, the road is once more clear, and the highest authority in the Church invites us all to walk in it'. In fact, less than a month before she signed the preface to her work, Pope Pius XII had issued his encyclical, *Divino Afflante Spiritu,* which one of the greatest Scripture scholars of the twentieth century, Raymond Brown, has described as a 'Magna Carta for biblical progress'.

This is not to suggest that her book is now found to be full of errors. In fact, it is astonishing that so little of what she wrote would now need to be revised in the light of modern scholarship. Many of the insights and comments in her book are still valid and uniquely hers.

However, many of the assumptions that she was justified in making at the time are no longer supported. For example, most scholars would now agree that St Paul was not the author of the Letter to the Hebrews, that Mark's gospel was earlier than Matthew's, and that Matthew's gospel was written in Greek, not translated from Aramaic. In this work it will be possible for us to draw on many more up-to-date resources than were available to her. This work is therefore not a further edition of Margaret Monro's book. The objectives and strategy of each may be similar, but the methods and contents of this work are my own.

Nor is it suggested that this book is a work of scholarship. In fact, another part of my motivation in writing it is that I hope, while doing so, to fill in some of the many gaps in my own knowledge. There is here no original research. The points of departure for what I write are *The New Jerome Biblical Commentary* edited by Raymond E Brown, Joseph A Fitzmyer and Roland E Murphy (NJBC) and *An introduction to the New Testament* by Raymond E Brown.

The work is therefore not adorned with scholastic footnotes. I have gained much from other works in addition to Brown's Introduction and the NJBC, especially those recommended for further reading in the final chapter. Readers who may wish to engage in further study should refer to those and other scholarly works.

I find that the first paragraph of Margaret Monro's preface expresses my aim and my limitations exactly:

> This little book is offered to those Catholics who would like to read the New Testament, but who find the available literature a trifle beyond them. Its purpose is to serve as a stepping stone to the better and fuller books which already exist. By making a selection only from the introductory material usually given, it

is hoped to provide an easier access to the text itself. Once the New Testament itself has been read with enough appreciation to ensure enjoyment, the fuller books become interesting and intelligible in quite a new way.

The Internet has brought another benefit, unimaginable to people in 1945. A vast storehouse of reference works is available at a few clicks of the mouse. You do not always have to go to a library. Where a reader with a healthy curiosity might wish to get more information about some statement made in the text, there may be a reference to a site that provides it. Simply click on the link and you should be connected. Even where I have not foreseen such a need, readers may conduct their own research online. You may find it convenient to bookmark *The Catholic Encyclopedia* as a starting point.

The Second Vatican Council in 1965 published its Dogmatic Constitution on Divine Revelation, *Dei Verbum,* which confirmed and carried forward the teaching and reforms of Pius XII. It included a specific exhortation to us, the laity.

> Likewise, the sacred Synod forcefully and specifically exhorts all the Christian faithful . . . to learn 'the surpassing knowledge of Jesus Christ' (Phil 3:8) by frequent reading of the Divine Scriptures. 'Ignorance of the Scriptures is ignorance of Christ.' Therefore let them go gladly to the sacred text itself. Let them remember, however, that prayer should accompany the reading of Sacred Scripture, so that a dialogue takes place between God and man. For, 'we speak to him when we pray, we listen to him when we read the Divine oracles'.
>
> *Dei Verbum* para. 25

A particular benefit that we may derive from a greater knowledge of the scriptures is that it should enhance our appreciation of and participation in the Sacred Liturgy of the Mass. The same Council, in its Constitution on the Sacred Liturgy, emphasised the connection.

> The two parts which, in a certain sense, go to make up the Mass, namely, the liturgy of the word and the eucharistic liturgy, are so closely connected with each other that they form but one single act of worship.
>
> *Sacrosanctum concilium,* Art. 56

In the introduction to the lectionary which contains the readings used at Mass we read:

> The church is nourished spiritually at the table of God's word and at the table of the Eucharist: from the one it grows in wisdom and from the other in holiness. In the word of God the divine covenant is announced; in the Eucharist the new and everlasting covenant is renewed. The spoken word of God brings to mind the history of salvation; the Eucharist embodies it in the sacramental signs of the liturgy
>
> Lectionary for Mass: Introduction #10

It is hoped that this small work may tempt many to be nourished more fully at the table of God's Word, while leaving unsatisfied a hunger and thirst for the deeper and more extensive knowledge to be gained from better and more scholarly works.

I have already acknowledged my debt to the *New Jerome Biblical Commentary* and to Raymond Brown's *Introduction to the New Testament*.

My principal indebtedness is to Dr Michele Connolly rsj, from whom I learned so much about the Greek language and the New Testament at the Catholic Institute of Sydney. I have done a bit of teaching at the tertiary level myself, so I can recognise a real expert when I see one. Her scholarship, realism and sense of fun made attendance at her lectures a pure joy. I am particularly grateful to her for encouraging me to persevere with writing and publishing this work, and for the great gift of her foreword, which endows on the work a legitimacy that it may not otherwise have enjoyed.

I have adopted her suggestion of using the modern scholarly convention of categorising dates as BCE (Before the Common Era) and CE (Common Era), rather than the old fashioned BC and AD that I grew up with, as many of my readers may have done.

I am grateful to Mary Jane Hogan and Leonie Turner, who read the whole manuscript, and Pat Dalton who read part of it, for their encouragement and suggestions.

Lastly, my friend of many years, scholar, teacher, author and editor, Janet Morrissey, has not only made numerous suggestions for improvement that I have been happy to accept, but has also meticulously imposed editorial consistency on my text, without which it would have been much more difficult to read and understand.

Alan Hogan

Introduction—How to use this book

This book is a plan for reading the books of the New Testament as a whole, mainly in the order in which they were written. What is important is the text of the New Testament itself. The purpose of this work is to convey basic information and background to each book, to enable readers to understand when, why and in what circumstances it was written, and what message the author intended to convey.

The order in which the books are read is important, especially for one reading the New Testament as a whole for the first time. They do not appear in our Bibles in the order in which they were written. For example, Paul's authentic letters preceded the gospels, especially that of John, and they appear, not in chronological order, but in the order of their length. Yet the books that make up the New Testament were written over a period of more than half a century, during which time Christ's followers developed and deepened their insights into the meaning and significance of his life, death and resurrection, and confronted a number of difficulties and emergencies. If we were to begin with Matthew 1:1 and read through to Revelation 22:21 we should lose all sense of the passage of time, the sequence of events and the development of doctrine.

Dates

Despite all the research that has been done, especially in the last half-century, scholars are still not able to fix the exact date of authorship of every book in the New Testament, though the broad outlines are reasonably clear. I have based the arrangement of chapters on the table of dates in Raymond Brown's article 'The canon of the New

Testament', in *The New Jerome biblical commentary*, p. 1045. That fact allows some flexibility, so that some books may be read out of what might be their strict time order if they are better read together. It also allows the arrangement to avoid too many consecutive heavy assignments. Nevertheless, after we have started with Acts, the rest of the books will be sufficiently in chronological order to suit our purposes.

In discussions in individual chapters I have adopted the dates suggested by Raymond Brown in *An introduction to the New Testament*. At this stage of our reading they are not particularly important in themselves. As Brown comments, 'Only rarely does a chronological difference have any theological import in reading Paul's letters', and 'I shall follow the traditional chronology both because it is the one that readers will most often encounter and because it seems more reasonable to me.'

Your readings

If you wish you could organise your readings into weeks, with each week usually devoted to one chapter. Chapters 1, 2 and 3 could be read in one week, as could chapters 5 and 6, 11 and 12, and 13 and 14. One reason is that the reading task assigned to each week should be easily achieved within that time, even for people as busy as we usually are. (Even the longest, the Gospels of Luke and Matthew, are only about thirty-five pages long in the New Revised Standard Version).

Assigning a specific time to a particular task that is both definite and achievable should help you to manage time. If you adhere to such a schedule you will be able to cover the whole of the New Testament in a little more than six months, which should be short enough to enable you to apprehend the entire project as a whole, while allowing sufficient time for reading to be reflective, rather than rushed.

Of course, especially if the work is being used by a single reader and not as part of a group, the timing may be flexible.

Some works, such as Matthew's gospel, may require much more time and attention than, say, 1 Peter. So far as the chronology permitted, I have therefore attempted not to assign too many heavy tasks in consecutive weeks. But there is no requirement to adhere strictly to any timetable. There is no magic in a week. A division into weeks is more a division into topics than a strict time schedule. If you find that you would like to take more time over any particular book, then do so.

Another reason for the arrangement into topics, is that the book should be suitable for use as a basis for discussion of the New Testament works as they are read by a group of friends who might meet regularly.

Which version?

Basically, for our present purposes, it does not much matter which of the many translations of the Bible you use. Some are more scholarly but stilted; others are written in a more modern and accessible style of English but may not be as accurate. We are not, however, embarking on an exercise in scholarship or academic learning.

Quotations in this work are taken from The Holy Bible: New Revised Standard Version (NRSV), which claims to be 'as literal as possible, as free as necessary'.

Others listed by Brown as relatively literal and therefore accurate are:
The New American Bible Revised Edition
The New International Version Bible
The Revised English Bible and
The New Jerusalem Bible—a study edition of this has a number of useful features.

Group Discussion

I have suggested that this work could be used as the basis for a Good News Book Club. A few suggestions for such a group follow:
- One person should be designated as the group leader for each session. It may be always the same person, or the role may be rotated among the members, but the leader in any session would have responsibility for what follows.
- Each meeting would begin with prayer. I suggest prayer to the Holy Spirit. We may always trust the Spirit to guide us, and under the Spirit's guidance we will be able to trust each other.

- The group should agree on the aim of the exercise. It is to enable us to know Jesus Christ the better. Its purpose is not academic, and the leader should help the group to avoid arguments about academic questions.
- The leader should encourage each member of the group to share their insights into what they have read during the previous week. No one member should dominate. No one should be left out.
- The group should agree on the time that each meeting should usually last. About an hour will often be suitable, but some may well wish to linger for longer over a particularly interesting topic, or even to spend more than one meeting on it.

Difficulties

Do not be surprised if you encounter difficulties in what you read. Even another Epistle writer found Paul difficult:

> So also our beloved brother Paul wrote to you according to the wisdom given him, speaking of this as he does in all his letters. There are some things in them hard to understand, which the ignorant and unstable twist to their own destruction, as they do the other Scriptures.
>
> 2 Peter 3:15

Do not be disturbed by them. This is not the time for solving them. Make a note of them, if you wish. Many may well be solved as you read more. But keep in mind that our objective is to experience the New Testament as a whole. When that has been done, resolving difficulties, or at least understanding them, will be much easier.

This exercise is much like the tourist's first guided tour on visiting a new city. The purpose is to get an overview, and to identify the places that one will wish to return to, time and time again, after getting some idea of the whole.

Keep a journal

You will add greatly to your enjoyment if you get into the habit of making a written note of things that occur to you as you read, and references to things that you discover on the way. Get a notebook. Always have the notebook and a pen with you as you sit down to read.

Prayerful reading

Reading the New Testament with the purpose of getting to know and love Jesus Christ the better is itself a prayerful activity. There is no need to clog it up with minor or formal devotional practices. All that is needed beforehand is a short period of recollection, putting aside the cares and concerns of the day, and a simple invocation of help from the Holy Spirit, the one who really inspired the writing that we are about to read. One could add a short prayer for help from the saint who actually wrote it.

If possible, read out loud. Paul's letters particularly were not newsletters, of which each member of the community received a copy, to be read privately and at leisure. Each community received one copy, which would be read aloud to all of them at their Eucharist. That is the sort of presentation that the author had in mind as he wrote.

Be aware of the different parts or phases of the letter or gospel that you are reading, and try to sum up what you think you learned in that part. Be alert also to the feelings that the writing arouses in you.

Then it would be simply good manners to finish with a prayer of thanksgiving for the help and insights we may have received.

Part 1 Origins of the New Testament

Chapter 1
The times, the places, the people

The life of Jesus encompassed about the first third of the first century CE.

> Note: Because mistakes were made during the Middle Ages in various reformations of the calendar, the birth of Christ is dated variously as between 8 BCE and 4 BCE.

He lived and taught entirely within the land we now know as Palestine, at the eastern end of the Mediterranean Sea. He died about 30 or 33 CE.

The political situation

When Alexander the Great extended his rule over Palestine in about 332 BCE, the Jews in Palestine, Syria and Egypt became part of the Hellenistic world. The process of translating the Hebrew Scriptures into Greek took place during the third century BCE.

> A legend that the task was carried out by a group of seventy-two elders led to its being called the Septuagint, or LXX (70 in Roman numerals). Citations of the Hebrew Scriptures in the New Testament documents are often from or close to the Septuagint version.

After the death of Alexander, the Seleucids ruled in the North and Ptolemies in the South. Their cruelty and persecutions led to a Jewish revolt by the Maccabees in 167 BCE, which lasted for 35 years.

Fig. 1.1

In about 135 BCE the Romans, who had defeated the Seleucids, recognised Jewish independence under the reign of the high priests, whose successors then squabbled for power so much that Rome intervened. Pompey entered Jerusalem and the temple in 63 BCE. The Romans then ruled the land through subservient high priests and minor kings.

After the civil wars that followed the assassination of Julius Caesar in 44 BCE, the Romans established the family of Herod as the local rulers. By 37 BCE Herod the Great had become undisputed king of Judea, though still subject to Rome. It was Herod the Great who, among other extensive building projects, built in Jerusalem a palace, the Fortress Antonia and the massive extension of the Temple, the destruction of which was to be foretold by Jesus (Mt 24:1-2; Mk 13:1-2; Lk 21:5-6). He was renowned for his brutal cruelty and suspicions, even murdering some of his own sons. He was quite capable of the slaughter of the innocents recorded in Mt 2:16-18.

Herod the Great died in 4 BCE. Resentment at his cruelty and greed erupted in a revolt. The Roman legate Varus descended from Syria with three legions and brutally crushed the rebellion. Two thousand Jews were crucified at Jerusalem. Augustus then split the realm among three of Herod's sons.

Antipas became tetrarch (minor ruler) of Galilee and Perea. Herod Antipas is the Herod most often referred to in the gospels. He continued to rule Galilee, from 4 BCE to 39 CE. It was he who ordered the beheading of John the Baptist in about 28 CE.

Philip was appointed tetrarch of the region north and east of the Lake of Galilee. Philip the Tetrarch rebuilt the city of Caesarea Philippi, calling it by his own name to distinguish it from the Caesarea on the seacoast, which was the seat of the Roman government.

Archelaus became ethnarc (governor of an ethnic community) in Judea, Samaria and Idumea. He so aroused the hatred of his people that they asked Rome to remove him. In 6 CE Augustus banished him to Gaul and made his territory the imperial province of Judea and appointed a procurator (sub-governor). Pontius Pilate held this position 26 CE to 36 CE. He sentenced Jesus to death in 30 or 33 CE.

> After Judea was made an imperial province a census was imposed for Roman tax purposes. A rebellion against this was led by Judas the Galilean and mentioned by Gamaliel in his speech to the council at Acts 5:37.

The grandson of Herod the Great, Herod Agrippa I gained control of what had been Philip's territory in 37 CE, and on the death of his father, Herod Antipas, he became king over Galilee also. From 41 to 44 he ruled over all Palestine, as had his grandfather. It was he who executed James, the brother of John, and arrested Peter, who escaped (Acts 12:1-19). His gruesome death is described in Acts 12:20-23.

At the death of Agrippa I in 44 CE, emperor Claudius sent procurators to rule Palestine as a Roman province. In 48 CE Agrippa II was given a small principality, which included the Temple. In 53 CE Claudius made him governor of the tetrarchy of Philip, and later added further territories to his rule. This is the Herod before whom Paul pleaded his cause at Caesarea Maritima, in about 59 CE (Acts 25:13-26:32).

The procurators appointed by Rome to rule Palestine in the period 44–66 were so corrupt and vicious that the people reacted, leading eventually to a widespread rebellion in 66 CE. It was ruthlessly suppressed by the Roman army under Vespasian. In 70 CE his son, Titus, sacked Jerusalem and completely destroyed the temple. Judaism ceased to be based on Temple worship. This event also played a pivotal role in the development of Christianity and its separation from Judaism.

The land

The land of the New Testament lay at the eastern end of the Roman Empire. It was divided into three main regions:

Centred on Jerusalem was Judea, the main southern part of the land, taking in the Dead Sea and the land between it and the Mediterranean.

To the north of Judea, extending as far as the Mt Carmel ridge which it included, was Samaria, which reached from the Mediterranean Sea and the Plain of Sharon on the west to the Jordan valley on the east

North of Samaria was Galilee, taking in the Lake of Galilee, and extending to the north, west and south west of the lake. The coastal plain to the west was the gentile land of Syro-Phoenicia. Galilee itself was divided into upper and lower Galilee.

Fig. 1.2
Landscape by the Sea of Galilee. Mount of Beatitudes in background

To the east and south east of the lake was the Greco-Roman area of Decapolis, so named because of its ten cities.

It is a small strip of land, only around 160 km (100 miles) from Capernaum in the North to the Southern end of the Dead Sea, say, the distance from Sydney to Newcastle in Australia, or New York to Philadelphia in USA. Today this area comprises the nations of Israel and Lebanon, the Palestinian homelands and, east of the River Jordan, the nation of Jordan.

Trade along the desert caravan routes meant that people were able to live in the sparse treeless plains of the Judean wilderness and the Negeb. The people in these regions would herd their flocks and till the soil if they could. Rich soil and good farming was possible on the great Plain of Megiddo, very close to Nazareth. In Jesus' time, and still today, many people lived along the shores of the freshwater Sea of Galilee.

The Jewish people

Jesus was born and raised a Jew; and died a Jew. This people traced their descent from Abraham. Their faith was founded on a belief in the one true God, who had made a series of covenants with them that he would be their God and they his people. The great prophet Moses had led their forefathers out of slavery in Egypt, and Solomon, son of David, had built the temple of God in Jerusalem, the holy city in the land that God had promised their ancestors. They believed that for their faithlessness they had been taken into slavery in Babylon, and then, by God's action, restored to their homeland, where the second Temple was rebuilt.

They lived by the Torah, the Law set out in the first five books of their sacred writings. Its features identified them as separate from all other nations, especially by male circumcision, observance of the Sabbath, food laws and purity ceremonies.

In Jesus' time traditional Jewish faith and religious observance was centred on the Temple in Jerusalem, with its daily rituals of prayer, sacrifice and burning of incense. Not everybody could get to the Temple regularly, and long before Jesus was born synagogues had developed in every Jewish region as gathering places for the people. Regular services of prayer and song were held in them. They were

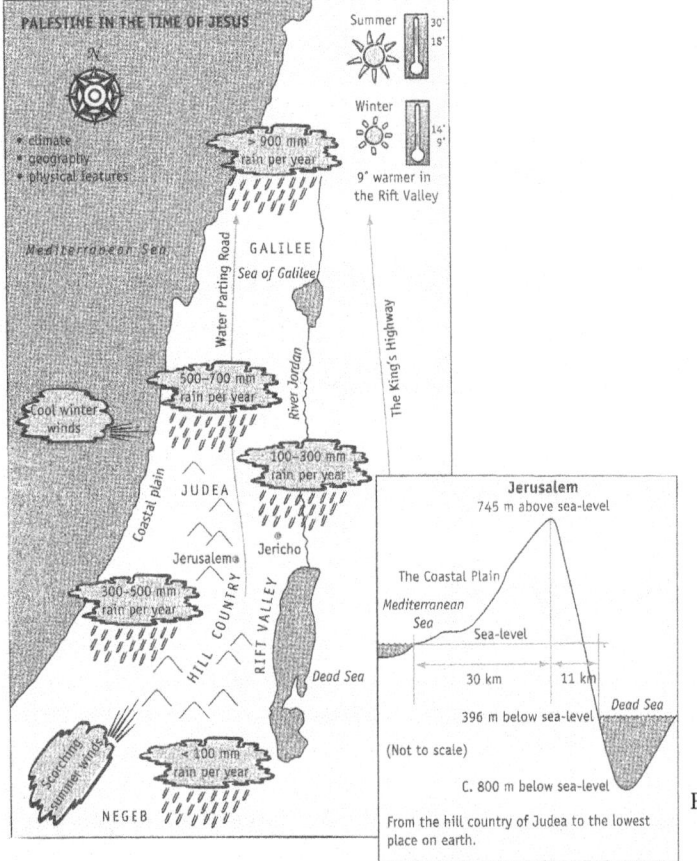

Fig. 1.3

places where the Torah was studied, and many had schools where boys were taught to read and write. The practice of preaching was developed in synagogues.

The original Greek term 'synagogue' meant an assembly or congregation of people. The synagogue could meet in an open space, a public square, under the trees or in a private house. In Jesus' time most were large rooms in private houses which eventually became public meeting places. Peter's house where Jesus stayed (Mark 1:29, 2:1) may have been such a place.

Priests and Levites

In second Temple Jerusalem (520 BCE—70 CE), the principal office in the Jewish community was that of the high priest. The high priest was not merely responsible for religious and spiritual life within the country, but was also chief administrator of internal secular policy, as well as the recognised representative of the Jewish community in all matters of external diplomacy. With the Roman conquest of Judea and subsequent Herodean rule, the office of high priest became a political tool in the hands of the administration, which became accustomed to deposing and appointing them. By Jesus' time there were, in addition to the ruling High Priest, a number of men who had formerly held the office, and they formed a separate class who continued to exercise great power in the council. With the destruction of the Temple, the office of High Priest vanished entirely from Jewish life.

The priests and Levites were the subordinate ministers appointed for the service of the tabernacle and the Temple. The Levites were so called because they were required to be of the tribe of Levi.

Significant groups in Jesus' time

The Pharisees were great students of the Law—the written Torah and the oral Torah. The Pharisees believed that God also gave Moses the knowledge of what these laws meant and how they should be applied. The oral Law was their attempt to interpret the Torah so that it could be adapted to the circumstances of everyday life. This oral tradition was codified and written down roughly three centuries later in what is known as the Talmud. They had great devotion to the Torah. Jesus shared many beliefs with the Pharisees, including beliefs about the resurrection of the dead, angels, alms-giving, prayer, fasting, addressing God as 'Father' and the importance of loving one's neighbour. They also believed in a messiah who would herald an era of world peace. There is a very negative image of the Pharisees in gospels. There is no evidence Jesus was a Pharisee. Paul, on the other hand, was undoubtedly one (Acts 23:6-8).

The Sadducees were the rivals of the Pharisees. They were elitists and had control of the Temple in Jerusalem. They wanted to maintain a priestly class but they were also liberal in their willingness to incorporate Roman culture into their lives, something the Pharisees opposed. The Sadducees rejected the idea of the oral Law and insisted on a literal interpretation of the written Law; consequently, they did not believe in an after life, and the existence of angels since they are not mentioned in the Torah. The main focus of Sadducee life were rituals associated with the Temple. The Sadducees disappeared around 70 CE, after the destruction of the Second Temple.

> These two 'parties' served in the Great Sanhedrin, a kind of Jewish Supreme Court made up of seventy-one members whose responsibility was to interpret civil and religious laws.

The Scribes were the professional interpreters of the Law. The prescriptions of the Law were very numerous and complicated, so that a class of people developed whose occupation was to study and expound it. Originally they had come from the ranks of the priests and Levites, but the priesthood lost much of its influence with the people by associating their fortunes with the foreign rulers, and the Scribes became differentiated from the priesthood. As a class they became narrow and exclusive, and tended to literal interpretation, legalism and subtle casuistry. They were the leaders of the Pharisees.

The Zealots were a political party of Jews as much as a religious one. They were a breakaway group from the Pharisees and they stuck solidly to the requirements of the Law. They were fierce opponents to the Roman rule of Palestine. Zealots who followed Jesus would have seen him as a military leader who would free the people from Roman domination.

Our knowledge of the Essenes is fragmentary and not particularly reliable. They appear to have been a sect that arose in the second century BCE in opposition to developments in the Temple and the corruption of the Temple priesthood by a succession of rulers. They were ascetical and tended to live in their own communities, apart from the ordinary people. It was a community of Essenes at Qumran who left the Dead Sea Scrolls. They do not figure in the New Testament. Suggestions that Jesus or John the Baptist were Essenes are fanciful.

The Samaritans, who occupied the region between Judea in the South and Galilee in the North, stood apart from mainstream Judaism. The Samaritans had a mixed Jewish and Assyrian ancestry and had developed their own compromised version of Judaism. They worshipped Yahweh, the one true God, but acknowledged only the Pentateuch.

> The Pentateuch consists of the first five books of the Hebrew Scriptures: Genesis, Exodus, Leviticus, Numbers and Deuteronomy.

Unlike the Jews, their ancestors had worshipped on Mount Gerazim instead of Mount Sion in Jerusalem. However, they believed that they could sacrifice to God outside the temple in Jerusalem. The Jews frowned on the Samaritans, denying that a non-Jew had any right to be included among the chosen people and angered that the Samaritans would dare to sacrifice to Yahweh outside of Jerusalem. Traditional Jews and Samaritans despised each other.

In the first century this Jewish religion was on a collision course with Roman imperial might. The glorification of the Emperor and the imperial standards clashed with the passionate belief of the Jews in a God whom no graven images could capture.

Added to this was the burden of taxation. The source of the great wealth enjoyed by the rulers and their associates was the agricultural labour of the people. Rome farmed out its taxes to the highest bidder, who was then authorised to extract the sum from the inhabitants of that province. The members or employees of these financial companies were the publicans mentioned in the gospels.

Taxes, however, had to be paid to the Temple as well as to Herod and to Rome, and the obligation to pay was ruthlessly enforced. The tax gatherer would extract his portion even from the threshing room floor. No wonder people were surprised when Jesus sat down to eat with the tax collectors and the publicans, who were the instruments of oppression of the ordinary people and the visible supporters of the hated idolatrous rulers.

Life in Nazareth

> For this section, I am indebted to Part 4 of the excellent book by American theologian, Elizabeth A Johnson, *Truly Our Sister: A Theology of Mary in the Communion of Saints*; New York: Continuum, 2006.

Jesus grew to maturity in the village of Nazareth, in southern Galilee. It was a small village, where the 300 to 400 people subsisted on agriculture. There were no signs of wealth. Only 6.5 km (4 m) away, on a high ridge to the northeast, was the Herodian city of Sepphoris, but Nazareth was off the road that led to that administrative centre. Sepphoris is not mentioned once in the New Testament. It is possible that Jesus, and perhaps Joseph, plied their trade there, as it was only about two hours walk away, but there is simply no evidence that he did so.

Nazareth was an insignificant village. One contemporaneous writer names forty-five Galilean villages, and another sixty-three, but neither of them mentions it.

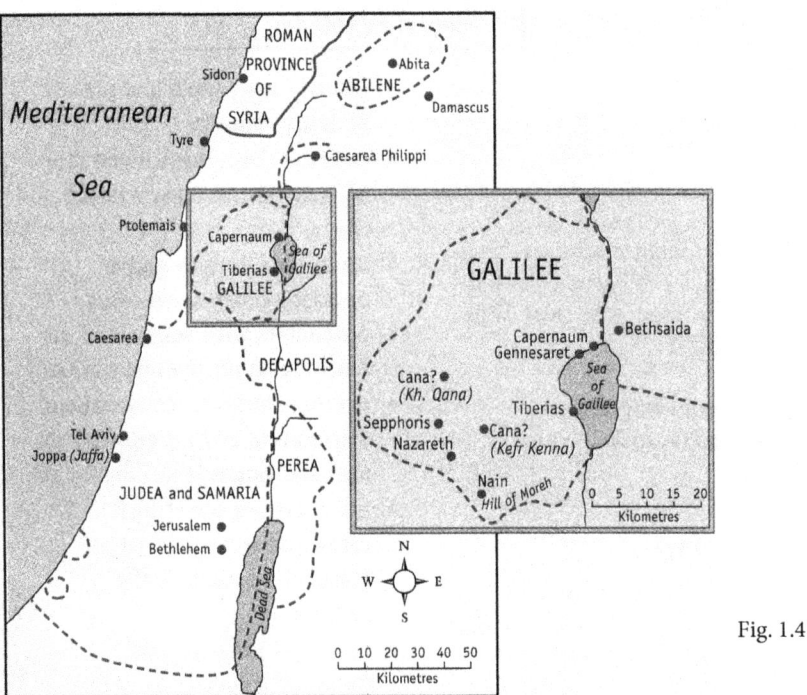

Fig. 1.4

When Philip told him about 'Jesus son of Joseph from Nazareth', Nathanael, himself a Galilean, replied, 'Can any thing good come out of Nazareth?' (John 1:46).

The inhabitants were farmers who worked their own land or as tenant farmers on land of another, and craftsmen who served their needs. Their dwellings were small and clustered together, each family having only one or two rooms, facing a communal walled courtyard.

Most English translations of Matthew 13:55 and Mark 6:3 describe Jesus as a carpenter. However, the Greek word *tekton* had a meaning wider than our modern concept of a skilled and specialised tradesman. It described a man who was accustomed to working on buildings, using stone as well as wood. He would also have made simple furniture, and agricultural implements such as ploughs. It was not an occupation that brought him any great social status. His own villagers disparaged him on account of it: 'Is not this fellow the *tekton* the son of Mary?' (Mk 6:3).

The Roman rulers spoke Latin, but the villagers would have had no contact with them. Greek was the language of the educated and ruling classes, such as the inhabitants of Sepphoris, but again the rural villagers would rarely have had occasion to communicate with them. There is no evidence that Jesus spoke Greek.

Hebrew was the ancient language of the Bible, which Jesus would have heard when the scrolls were read at the synagogue. There are many places in the gospels where Jesus is depicted as having a deep and wide acquaintance with the Hebrew Scriptures.

However, the ordinary, everyday language of the people was Aramaic, which was related to Hebrew as one of the Semitic family of languages. The two languages shared the same script and alphabet, and had many words in common. Aramaic had for some time been the lingua franca of the whole region. We must bear in mind when we read the gospels that when the evangelist is reporting what Jesus said, the report is of a translation from Aramaic into Greek.

While Jesus was being tried in the house of Caiaphas, the High Priest, the bystanders were able to distinguish Peter as a Galilean by his accent (Mt 26:73). We may assume that Jesus also would have been perceived by the sophisticated inhabitants of Jerusalem as a country yokel.

His parents brought Jesus up as an observant Jew. He was circumcised (Lk 2:21), and presented to the Lord in the temple as prescribed by the Law of Moses (Lk 2:22-24). He was taken to Jerusalem each year for the feast of the Passover (Lk 2:41). The cloak *(tallit)* he wore had tassels *(tzitzit)* on it, as prescribed by the Law. It was his custom to attend the synagogue at Nazareth on the Sabbath (Lk 4:16), and the evangelists, especially Luke, depict him from the outset of his ministry as being thoroughly familiar with the Hebrew Scriptures.

Chapter 2
The manuscript evidence

Christianity was not founded on a book. It was founded on the faith of his followers in Jesus of Nazareth. His resurrection from the dead vindicated him, as Messiah and Son of God, and his message of the imminent coming of the Reign of God. This faith spread, and then many documents were later written about it. Later still, over a period of centuries, the church gradually chose those writings which it regarded as having a special place in its worship and doctrine, and which it regarded as having been inspired by God. These are what we now call the New Testament.

> Old Testament or Hebrew Scriptures? It has become more common to use Hebrew Scriptures to underline that there is nothing 'old' (past its use-by date) about the Hebrew Scriptures. For Jews, and indeed for Christians, the Hebrew Scriptures continue to be the living treasury of God's Word.

In the first period of the Church's history, immediately following the resurrection and ascension, there were no specifically Christian writings. 'Scripture' meant to the apostles and the disciples what it had meant to Jesus, namely The Law, the Prophets and the Writings that made up the Written Torah, or what Christians came to call the Old Testament.

The earliest Christians found out about Jesus from the oral preaching of the apostles, and then of other disciples. Although they used the Written Torah to support and confirm their message (see, eg 2 Tim 3:16–17 and 2 Pet 1:19–21), those Scriptures did not constitute the basis of their teaching. Judaism had not yet finally decided which particular works constituted inclusively and exclusively its sacred books. Nowhere in them was it foretold that the Messiah would suffer and die and be raised again. They could not form the basis of Christianity. Gentile converts were not always familiar with the Hebrew Scriptures.

Over the rest of the first century CE, as the apostles died and Christianity spread further and further from Jerusalem, the dissipation of the oral tradition led to the need for the composition of Christian writings, especially to confront difficulties that arose in particular Christian communities. There had come into existence some collections of the sayings of Jesus, and other materials that are now lost to us, but which were used by Christian writers, together with the oral tradition, especially for the composition of the Gospels. Practically all that we now include in the New Testament had been written by the end of the first century.

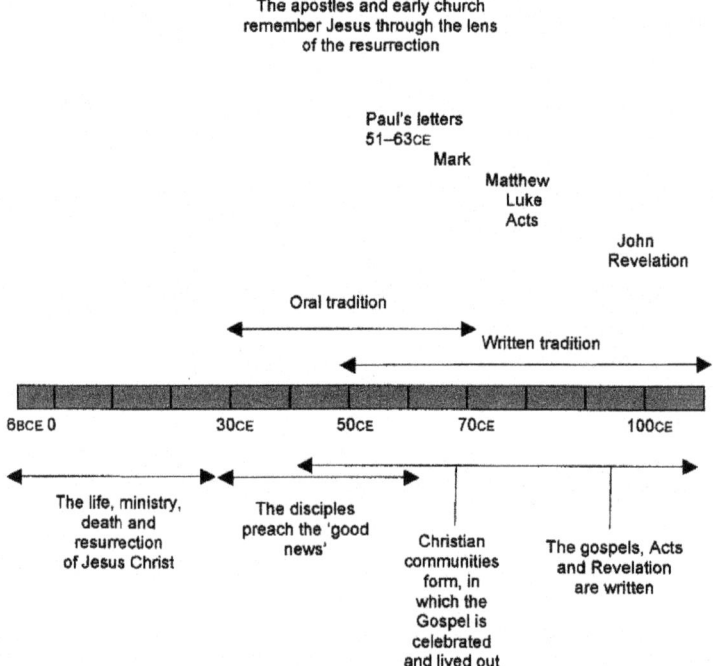

Fig. 2.1
The formation of the New Testament

Scholars have not been able to fix the dates of composition of most of the New Testament with any great accuracy. Except for the early letters of St Paul, their estimates vary with an approximation of about a decade. 2 Peter may have been as late as 100+. Where it may help understanding, more detailed comment about the date of each work may be made as each is introduced.

The writing materials then in use were papyrus and parchment. Papyrus was made in Egypt. It was a good, relatively cheap material, but it became brittle with age. Sheets of papyrus could be glued together to form a scroll, which would be wound on a stick to form a volume, up to 10.6 m (35 ft) in length. The whole of the Gospel of Luke might fit on such a scroll, but not much more. Obviously finding one's place in such a volume could be inconvenient, as it might mean unrolling practically the whole scroll. From early in the second century pages were sewn together, much as in a modern book, called a codex. As the technology developed, a codex could contain much more than a scroll. Some of the oldest surviving Christian works come from papyrus codices.

Animal skins had been used as writing materials from very ancient times. During the second century BCE the process of production, using mainly sheepskin, was greatly enhanced in the city of Pergamon, (an ancient Greek city in what is now Turkey), from which parchment gets its name. A finer grade of the material came from using calfskin, and was called vellum (Latin, *vitellus,* a little calf, cf. English *veal*), though this word later came to be used of other finer types of parchment. Parchment was originally more expensive than papyrus, but when the reed beds in Egypt became worked out, papyrus no longer had any economic advantage. The durability of parchment also made it more suitable for books that were meant to be read over and over, so that the major biblical codices were copied onto parchment. Sometimes an earlier writing could be scraped or washed off, and the skin reused for a later writing. Technology can uncover the earlier writing. Such documents are called palimpsests.

> A small fragment of the most ancient papyrus manuscript of parts of Acts Ch 2, dated to mid-third century, is located in the Department of Ancient History at Macquarie University in Sydney

Not one of the original documents of the New Testament has been preserved. The earliest copy of a New Testament book yet found is a small scrap of papyrus on which are inscribed four verses of John 18. It has been dated to about 125 CE (±25 years), and was published in 1935.

On the basis of the type of writing used, the texts are usually categorised as uncial or minuscule. Uncial (Latin *uncia*, an inch) were the formal upright block letters separated from each other, like modern capitals, commonly used in ancient literary works. In everyday documents, a more cursive script with smaller letters developed over time, and is called minuscule. It became common for biblical copies after the ninth century.

> A New Testament minuscule is a copy of a portion of the New Testament written in a small, cursive Greek script

Before the many discoveries that have been made since about 1890, the oldest copies of the Greek New Testament available to scholars were the Great Uncial codices of the fourth and fifth centuries. These often also contained parts of the Greek version of the Hebrew Scriptures. About 260 distinct uncial manuscripts of the Greek New Testament have survived, but the four most important for New Testament studies were as follows (they are conventionally identified by a capital letter).

Codex Vaticanus (B). This has been dated to the mid-fourth century. It is located in the Vatican Library. It is probably the oldest of the Great Codices, but the New Testament is incomplete.

Codex Sinaiticus ℵ or (S). ℵ is aleph, the first letter of the Hebrew alphabet. This is also from the mid-fourth century. It was discovered by a series of lucky chances in 1859 in the Monastery of St Catherine in the Sinai Peninsula. It is of similar antiquity to B, but the New Testament is complete, hence the claim on the websites that it is the oldest complete bible. The bulk of it is in the British Library. The story of its discovery, and how it finished up there, is fascinating, and is told by Metzger in *The text of the New Testament*, 42-4

Codex Alexandrinus (A). Dated to the early fifth century, this codex is now in the British Library

Codex Bezae (D). This codex was named after Theodore Beza, who in 1581 donated it to the University of Cambridge, where it is now kept. It is dated to the fifth or sixth century, and is in both Greek and Latin.

Fig. 2.2.
Page from *Codex Vaticanus*; ending of 2 Thes and beginning of Hebrews. Note that the letters simply fill each line; there is no spacing between words, no punctuation and no division into paragraphs or numbering of verses. These were later refinements. The script is uncial.

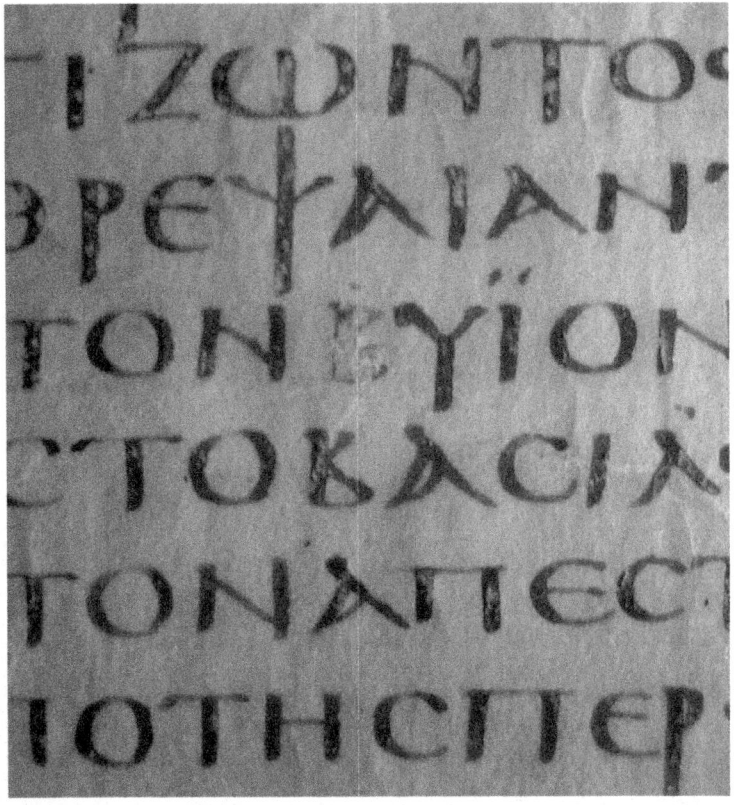

Fig 2.3
Codex Sinaiticus: Erasure on Quire 40, folio 2 recto. 1 Maccabees, Chapter 6. Project website [www.codexsinaiticus.org/en/] features all extant pages of the Codex.

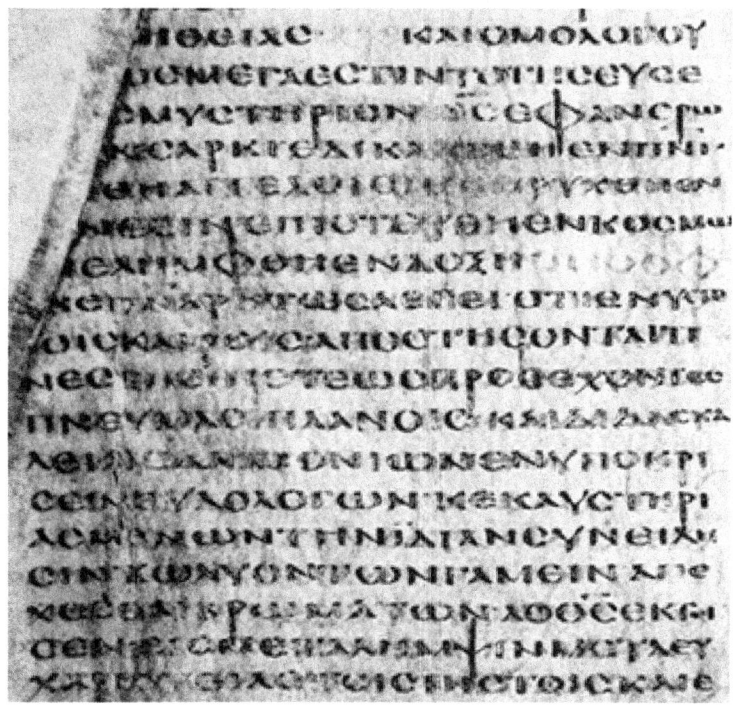

Fig 2.4
The text of 1 Timothy 3:16–4:3 from Codex A, as presented in the photographic facsimile volume published by the British Museum in 1879.

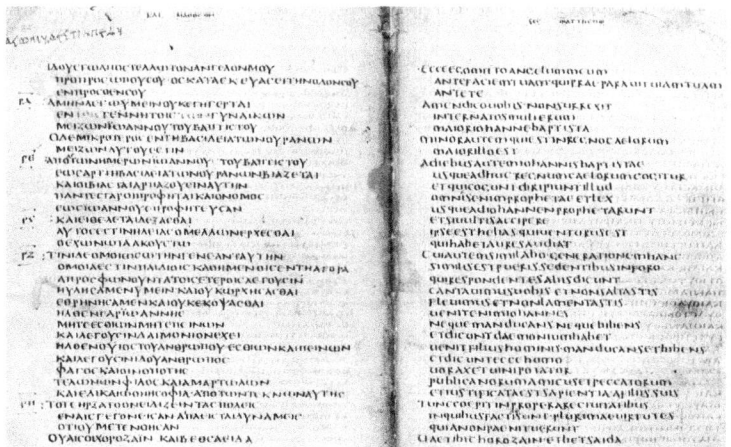

Fig. 2.5
Codex Bezae Cantabrigiensis, Matthew 11:10-21. The Greek text is on the left hand page and the Latin on the right. It contains only the four Gospels and the Acts.

After the invention of cursive writing in the ninth century the number of minuscule copies rapidly increased. Some 2,800 minuscule manuscripts are known.

Of course, not all copyists were of equal skill, and none were perfect, so that there are many differences in detail in all those many copies. They were carried over into the books that were produced following the invention of printing, such as the first published Greek New Testament produced by Erasmus in 1516. Beza, the owner of D, published a number of editions of the Greek New Testament between 1565 and 1598, on the basis of which the brothers Elzevir published a text, in the preface to which in 1633 they spoke of the *textum nunc ab omnibus receptum*—'the text now received by all'—hence the name *Textus Receptus*.

The claim to unanimity could not last. Earlier codices became available. After 1890 some ninety papyrus manuscripts of New Testament books had been discovered, especially in Egypt with its dry climate. Translations from the Greek into the old Latin and old Syriac languages, as well as Coptic, Armenian, Georgian and Ethiopic, had been made and were discovered, some dating from the end of the second century and the third century, antedating the Great Uncial Codices by 200 years. For the Vulgate edition of the Bible, St Jerome had not only translated the Jewish Scriptures from Hebrew sources but in about 383–4 CE, he had produced a version of the Gospels translated from the Old Latin in the light of good Greek manuscripts. The remaining Vulgate books of the New Testament were produced shortly afterwards in the same tradition.

> It is called Vulgate because after St Jerome's work in reconciling the many versions that then existed, it became the standard text used by the church. The Latin *vulgare* means 'to make generally accessible'.

Fig. 2.6
Cave IV at Qumran. Although no complete scrolls were found in this cave, the fragments found were by far the most important.

In and after 1947 some complete manuscripts and thousands of fragments of scrolls were found in caves at and near Qumran, on the northwest shore of the Dead Sea. They did not include any Christian or New Testament documents, but they were written in Hebrew, Aramaic and Greek, and included Hebrew and Greek copies of parts of the Written Torah and other Jewish literature. They contributed greatly to our understanding of Judaism from about 150 BCE to 70 CE, a period that included the beginnings of Christianity, and therefore to our understanding of the background to the writing of the New Testament documents.

In the twentieth century it became possible to use all these materials in a truly scientific manner, using the analytical tools of history, archaeology, palaeography and other sciences. A series of scholarly editions of the Greek New Testament were published, involving cooperation from a number of Bible Societies and scholars from the Catholic and Protestant traditions. This work continues.

Finally, Raymond Brown comments, 'It is worth noting that the different readings, as numerous as they are, do not touch on any essential questions of Christian faith. In terms of the number of early copies preserved and of fidelity in copying, the New Testament is remarkable, especially when compared with the masterpieces of Greco-Roman literature'.

Chapter 3
The evolution of the canon

The word 'canon' is used in many senses. In Greek its primary meaning was a reed, or a straight rod. It came to mean a standard, a rule, or a norm.

Early Christian writers used the word to refer to a rule of faith, or truth. Later it came to be used as meaning a list, as when a saint is 'canonised' by being included in the list of those held up by the church as exhibiting exemplary virtue.

The developed usage that is important for our purposes is that the church came to recognise a certain group of writings that provided the standard for faith and life, and those books came to be included in a list called the canon.

Both in the Catholic and the Protestant tradition, the same list of twenty-seven works is nowadays included in the canon of the New Testament.

There were, however, other works written by the middle of the second century that purported to recount the sayings and doings of Jesus, but which for various reasons have not been included in the canon. These works are referred to as apocryphal, or hidden.

In one collection of Christian apocrypha over 100 works are listed. Some are patterned on the letters of Paul, or on the acts of various apostles, such as the Acts of Thomas or the Acts of John. More were designated as gospels, sometimes developing particular aspects of Jesus, such as his infancy and birth, his sayings, his passion and resurrection, or post-resurrection dialogues. Examples are the Gospel of Thomas or the Gospel of Peter.

History, however, is virtually silent about the details of the process by which the canonical list has been derived, when and by whom. The process extended over centuries. It is too complex for discussion in detail here.

There was no deliberate decree by any person or Council at the beginning of the Christian era specifying which works were canonical and which were not. Instead there was a long and continuous process, not only of collecting, but also of sifting and rejecting.

Neither was there any agreed single criterion for inclusion or rejection. Different factors operated at different times and in different places. Nevertheless, eventually a number of works became recognised as sacred and authoritative, and placed on the same level as the Hebrew Scriptures.

One important criterion for inclusion was a real or putative apostolic origin. Paul undoubtedly wrote a number of the letters attributed to him. Others were written by followers in his name and assuming his authority. The gospels of John and Matthew were attributed to those apostles, and those of Mark and Luke to companions of Peter and Paul. Other works, however, that bore the name of an apostle were rejected and became apocryphal.

The importance and experience of the particular community to which a work was addressed often played a significant role in its acceptance.

Most important was conformity with the rule of faith, the standard beliefs of the Christian communities. Works perceived as heretical were excluded.

One of the influences at work was the practice of reading and referring to apostolic works at the Eucharist in various churches, and then their translation into other languages, such as Latin, Syriac and Coptic.

During periods of persecution believers were forced to decide which books were scripture, to be hidden from the authorities, and which were not, to be surrendered without guilt. The development of codices enabled works that formerly would have been recorded on separate rolls to be collected in one bound volume.

By the end of the fourth century there was broad, though not universal, agreement on a list of twenty-seven works. In a festal letter published at Easter 367 CE Athanasius contrasted the twenty-seven books included by him in the *canon* with those deemed apocryphal. The lists used were becoming more uniform and acquiring Episcopal approval. A basic list was endorsed by the Councils of Hippo (393 CE), Carthage III (397 CE) and Carthage IV (419 CE).

During the Reformation disputes had arisen about the authority of some works, and in 1546 the Council of Trent endorsed the canon of twenty-seven works that we now have, 'so that no doubt may remain as to which books are recognised'.

Part 2 **Reading the New Testament**

Chapter 4
The Acts of the Apostles

There are a number of reasons why we begin with Acts.

It is such a well-told story. Luke is a prince of storytellers, and he put a great deal of skill and effort into polishing his work. It is full of incident—murder, escapes from prison, earthquake, shipwreck, conflicts with authority, even disagreements within the church (yes, even then!).

It is the beginning of our own story, of our church, telling how the followers of Jesus carried out his command to be his 'witnesses in Jerusalem, all Judea and Samaria and to the ends of the earth', a command that is still addressed to us.

It is necessary for us to have an overview of this part of our story in order to understand the rest of the New Testament, especially the letters of St Paul.

Paul played a vital role in this story, not only by what he did during his apostolate, but also by the influence his letters have since had on the development and enrichment of doctrine. We read about his journeys to the communities to whom he wrote his letters, how he was received there, and why he had the obvious affection for them that so illuminates his letters.

He was probably born during the first decade of the first century CE, in Tarsus, the capital city of the Roman province of Cilicia, in what is now southern Turkey. At that time Jews in that city could receive Roman citizenship, and Paul claimed to be a Roman citizen from birth. In his own letters he used the name Paulos, the Greek form of a well-known Roman family name. In Acts, Luke at first refers to him as Saulos, a Semitic form of the name, though from Acts 13:9 he also uses Paulos.

He grew up and was educated in Jerusalem as an observant Jew, in accordance with the Law. He proclaimed himself a Pharisee (Phil 3:5–6), and Luke reports him as stating to Herod Agrippa that he had voted in the Sanhedrin for the death of the followers of Jesus, which would indicate that he was also a rabbi (Acts 26:10).

It is probable that he had been married, as it would be most unusual for a Pharisee not to be, and marriage was a requirement for a rabbi. Another possible clue is in his letter to the Philippians, where he asks his 'loyal companion' (singular and no names) to help Euodia and Syntache. The Greek phrase literally meant 'yoked together', and was frequently used of those united by marriage, though it could also indicate other close relationships. Some scholars suggest that he may have been widowed.

Luke finishes his description of Paul's travels with him in Rome, effectively under house arrest, continuing his mission 'at the end of the earth'. Tradition holds that he was martyred by beheading towards the end of Nero's persecutions, in about 69 CE.

By the time Luke wrote Acts, Peter and Paul had probably been martyred and the Romans had destroyed the temple. But the events about which he writes had happened before then, and before much of the rest of the New Testament was written.

> Note: We will read Acts again later, concentrating on its theology.

Luke did not write Acts primarily as a history book in the modern sense. It was just as much a theological treatise as was his gospel, and he chose his materials and arranged them so as best to make his theological points. But Acts is as close as we get in the New Testament to what we would understand as history. Its stories are founded on real events, even though the book is stylised, and not completely accurate in all its details. Sometimes, for example, Luke will differ from Paul in some particular. Naturally, when that happens, we would be inclined to accept the direct evidence of Paul, unless some other evidence satisfies us to the contrary.

Note the passages where the story changes from 'he' or 'they' to 'we'. They seem to indicate that for part of the time Luke accompanied St Paul. Scholars are not united in their opinions about this, but I follow those who think that he did. There is no particular pattern that I can discern in the occasions on which the changes take place to explain them otherwise. Their very randomness inclines me to think that Luke is telling the simple truth.

Another suggestion is to note the occasions on which the Spirit plays a part in the story.

If you are not able to read the whole book at one sitting, it falls naturally into three unequal parts.

Chapters 1—8:1a tell of the beginning of the Church's mission, in Jerusalem, where Peter is the main protagonist. The level of violence in the reaction of the authorities increases, until it results in the death of Stephen. We first meet Paul.

Chapters 8:1b—12:25 recount the mission in the rest of Judea and Samaria, in which others are involved, but in which Peter is still prominent, and the conversion of Paul.

The rest of the book is nearly all about Paul, first on his mission with Barnabas, converting gentiles, and obtaining approval to do so at Jerusalem. Then there is his mission to the ends of the earth, finishing in Rome, but implying, 'To be continued', which is where we now are.

On the basis of Luke's description it is conventional to list Paul's travels as three missionary journeys and a final journey to Rome. It is apparent from his letters, however, and even from Acts itself (e.g. 18:22–23), that he travelled more extensively and revisited more

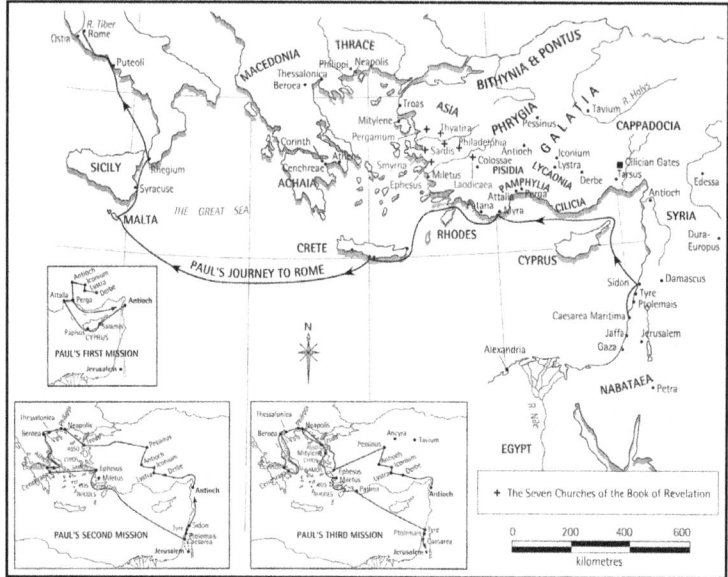

Fig. 4.1
Paul's missionary journeys

cities than this convention would indicate. Nevertheless, it will help to understand the letters that will be discussed in detail later to pay careful attention to the journeys as described in Acts.

In the **first journey** the Antioch church sent Barnabas and Paul to Cyprus and nearby Asia Minor (13:1—14-28).

The **second journey** began with Paul's separation from Barnabas. At first, now with Silas, he went through Syria and his native Cilicia, Phrygia and Galatia, to Troas on the western coast of Asia Minor. There he received the call to go over to Macedonia (modern Greece). He travelled through a number of cities to the south of Greece, especially Corinth, eventually returning via Ephesus to Jerusalem and then back to Antioch (15:36—18:22) where Paul stayed a while.

In the **third journey**, Paul again set out through Galatia and Phrygia to Ephesus, where he stayed for two years. He eventually decided to travel again through Greece, to Jerusalem and then on to Rome (18:23—19:22). After the famous riot of the silversmiths in Ephesus, Paul returned to Greece, as he had intended, and revisited the churches there. After leaving Greece he rejoined his companions at Assos, a port on the west coast of Asia Minor. From there he sailed down the coast to Miletus where he met the elders from the church of Ephesus and bade them an emotional farewell. From Miletus he took ship for Israel, arriving eventually in Jerusalem, to be greeted warmly by the church there (20:1—21:17).

After his arrest in Jerusalem, Paul was taken in custody to Caesarea, for a trial before Felix the governor, and was in custody there for two years until Festus replaced Felix as governor. Before Felix he appealed to the Emperor (25:11).

Eventually, still a prisoner, he was put on board a ship that was about to sail from Caesarea to ports along the coast of Asia Minor. They went north to Sidon, and then on to Myra (now southern Turkey), where Paul was transferred to another ship bound for Italy. The season for safe sailing was ending, and they were driven north towards Cnidus, and then south to Fair Havens in Crete— 'the harbour was not suitable for spending the winter' (27:12).

Despite Paul's misgivings, they set out from Crete, eventually being shipwrecked on Malta. Three months later they sailed, first to Syracuse in Sicily, called in at Rhegum on the southern tip of Italy, and eventually landed at Puteoli on the western coast of Italy, from where they travelled overland to Rome (27:13—28:16).

There are two main sources for our knowledge about Paul—what Luke wrote about him, and what he wrote himself, in his letters. It will be helpful, as we read the letters, to recollect when and how and why he first met the people to whom he was writing. But it is even more important to form a picture, from what Luke writes, about what sort of a man he was, and why he wrote as he did. Keep that in mind as you read the second half of Acts.

- *Now, plan your time, get down your copy of the New Testament, your pen and your notebook, and begin to read...*

- *Did you notice the part that the Holy Spirit played in the early Church? How does that compare with our attitudes and practice today?*

Chapter 5
The letters of Paul

Before we begin the first of Paul's letters, there are a number of matters relating to all of them that must be discussed.

> Note: For what follows I am indebted, not only to Raymond Brown's Introduction, but also to the presentations by Fr Brendan Byrne SJ and Sr Michele Connolly during the Year of St Paul eConference, broadcast by the Broken Bay Institute on 30 June 2009.

Did Paul write them all?

There are thirteen letters in all and scholars are now generally agreed that the letters attributed to Paul in the Bible fall into three categories.

Seven of them are almost universally agreed to be the authentic letters of Paul himself:
1 Thessalonians
Galatians
Philippians
Philemon
1 and 2 Corinthians, and
Romans.
Next is a group of three, which many scholars (though not all) think were written in his name by his followers shortly after his death in Rome in about 64 CE. They are:
Colossians
Ephesians, and
2 Thessalonians. As a group they are referred to as the Deutero-Pauline epistles. (Deutero means 'second'.)

Lastly there are the three pastoral letters written in his name at a much later stage in the development of the church, and they reflect the different situation that the church then faced. They are:
1 Timothy
2 Timothy, and
Titus.
They are called pseudonymous.

The letter to the Hebrews is not now listed in our Bibles as being from Paul, but for many years it was thought that it was. As will be seen when we come to discuss it, modern scholarship does not include it among Paul's works.

Many of the criticisms that are made, for example about Paul's attitude to women, are based on statements made in those later epistles, or in an interpolation added by a copyist to an authentic letter.

> Note: Paul and women will be discussed later, when we have read more of what Paul actually wrote.

These statements form part of the canon of the New Testament, and they must be interpreted accordingly, but a false picture of Paul is painted by attributing to him views that he did not himself express.

How to read a Pauline letter

In understanding anything in the New Testament, context is most important. When we read one of Paul's letters we need to be aware that the letter is only one part of an ongoing relationship with the community to which he is writing. These letters are largely written to 'churches' which he had visited and address the particular needs of the early Christian communities to which they are addressed. For example:

- The Thessalonian community is apparently anxious and confused in his absence; they receive a letter of consolation and comfort (1 Thess: 2.17—5.28).
- The Galatian community seems ready to reject Paul entirely and become much more Jewish in their orientation; like a scolding parent,

he berates them and tells them that they cannot turn back on the Gospel of Christ that he had given them (Galatians: 1.6–24; 2.1–2,14; 3.1—5.26).
- The Corinthian community is suffering from too much division and strife; he writes a letter of instruction on harmony and unity (1 Cor: 1.10–17).
- The Roman community comprised many Jews as well as gentiles and it is probable Paul's Letter to the Romans was written in preparation for his journey to Rome. Paul is aware there is some conflict between gentile and Jewish Christians in the Roman church and so he attempts to reconcile the apparent rejection of Jesus by Israel with fulfilment of God's covenants with them, and the incorporation of the gentiles into the 'new Israel' (chapters 9, 10 and 11).

Next, we will see that there is a consistent pattern in his letters, and in their division into parts. Naturally he was following the conventions of his times. A Greco-Roman letter tended to follow a set format, and ignorance of that format can lead to misinterpretation.

Usually there were four parts to a letter:

In the opening formula Paul first identifies himself as the writer, and often mentions others who were with him. He usually identifies himself as an apostle, or as a servant of or prisoner for Jesus Christ.

> Paul, Silvanus, and Timothy

Next he names the community to whom the letter is addressed.

> To the church of the Thessalonians in God the Father and the Lord Jesus Christ

Then he invariably invokes for his readers grace and peace, in all but one case (1 Thess) from God the Father and Jesus Christ.

> Grace to you and peace.

Peace (*eirene* in Greek) was for Paul a word rich in connotation. It implied being in a normal state, as distinct from being in a state of confusion, that is, having peace of soul. It also meant to be at peace with God and with one another.

In all but one case (Galatians) Paul then gives thanks to God for some gift that God has given to his readers, reminding them that God is a God of grace.

> We always give thanks to God for all of you in our prayers, constantly remembering before God our Father your work of faith and labor of love and steadfastness of hope…

Then follows the body of the letter. Often, in the early part, he may speak of some important aspect of the way God relates to us in Christ. Then he addresses matters that concern that community at the time, and advises them about how they should live, because of that relationship. He is eloquent in trying to connect with them, often using quite emotional language.

Finally, there is the conclusion, where he sometimes has a personal message to or from his co-workers, or his own signing of the letter. Often he again wishes the community peace, but invariably there is a prayer for them that they may have the grace of God.

> Now may the Lord of peace himself give you peace at all times in all ways. The Lord be with all of you.

Grace, as Paul uses the word, is the free gift that God, the lovable and loving God, gives to us. It is the gift of reconciliation to Himself, or salvation, made actual in the life, death and resurrection of Jesus Christ.

> Grace (*charis* in Greek) is a central concept in Paul's theology. It first means the beauty or charm that makes a person lovable (charismatic). It then comes to mean a gift that is the expression of that charm.

Paul attributed his own conversion to the grace of God (1 Cor 15:9–10). He developed this idea of grace in detail in a number of his letters, but at the beginning of every letter that he wrote he expresses his desire that his listeners should receive it.

Chapter 6
1 Thessalonians

- Quickly review chapters 15 and 16 of Acts

Luke uses the name 'Silas', the Greek form of a Jewish name, but in Paul's letters he is called by his Latin name Silvanus.

We met Silas, who was the 'leader among the brothers' and 'prophet' who had been sent with Paul, Barnabas and Judas to Antioch with the letter containing the decision of the Council at Jerusalem (Acts

Fig. 6.1

15:22-32). They set out to revisit the churches they had founded in what is now Turkey, on what is conventionally referred to as Paul's second missionary journey (Acts 15:36-41).

At Lystra Paul was joined by Timothy, who was to play such an important part in the rest of his apostolate (Acts 16:1-5). At Troas Paul received the call to cross over to Macedonia, which then was the northern part of modern Greece.

After a stormy time in Philippi, where Paul was shamefully treated, but demonstrated that he was not a man to be trifled with, they came to Thessalonica, about 161 km (100 miles) west on the great Roman road across the north of Greece, the Via Egnatia. There they proclaimed the Gospel, with some success. Thessalonica was an important port city, and capital of the Roman province of Macedonia. (It is today the second largest city in Greece.) The Jewish population was substantial enough to have its own synagogue. Some of the converts were Jews, who had encountered Paul when he expounded the Scriptures in their synagogue (Acts 17:1-4); others were gentiles, who had turned to God from the idols that they had worshipped (1 Thess 1:9-10; 4:3-6).

It is not clear how long he stayed there, as a guest in the house of Jason (Acts 17:5-9), but he was there long enough to have received financial help more than once from the church at Philippi (Philippians 4:16). While there he worked day and night so as not to be a burden on the Thessalonians (1 Thess 2:9). However, it was not long before he was forced to make another hasty departure first to Beroea and then to Athens (Acts 17:10-15).

> 1 Thessalonians is probably the first of the documents that were to form the New Testament. It was written about 50 or 51 CE, less than twenty years after the Ascension.

He may well have felt that he had not been with them long enough to tell them all that he wanted to, and he was worried about the effect that persecution might have on them. He wanted to return to them, but could not, so he sent Timothy to them, to strengthen and encourage them.

From Athens, meanwhile, Paul went on to Corinth, where Silas and Timothy eventually rejoined him (Acts 18:5), bringing the good news that the Thessalonians were holding firm. Paul then sent this letter from the three of them.

Timothy had brought back news that while he was with the Thessalonians one topic kept coming up that was worrying them. They had been told that Jesus had said that he would return, and they looked forward to the coming of the Lord. They and Paul knew that Jesus had not said when he would come, but none of them would have been contemplating a wait of more than 2000 years—it was an event that they all expected to happen soon. But even since Paul had been with them some who had believed in Christ had died. 'What would the Lord do about them? What if any of us die before he comes?'

Paul sets out to reassure them. First he recalls to them what he had already taught them, to put aside their former lustful life as pagans (4:1-8). Then he deals with the problem. God, through Jesus, will bring with him those who have died (4:14). Even Paul expects that he may still be alive when the Lord comes (4:15), but no one knows when that will be. Nor does it matter, so long as they keep to their faith, hope and love (5:8). He concludes the letter with some pastoral advice, and a blessing, and his invariable invocation of Christ's grace for them.

> The term 'pagan' is derived from the Latin *pagus*, a village, whence *pagani* (i.e. those who live in the country), a name given to the country folk who remained heathen after the cities had become Christian.

- Note throughout the letter the tenderness and emotion with which Paul writes. There is very little admonition but quite a lot of praise and even flattery, praise for what they had done and encouragement to do more.

- Note also Paul's command at 5:26. When would be a suitable occasion for the letter to be read to all the brethren? Surely at their Eucharist—thus began our liturgical tradition of listening at Mass to readings from the epistles.

Raymond Brown in his *Introduction* (p. 465) writes that in this, the earliest Christian writing, within the opening ten verses there are references to God the Father, the Lord Jesus Christ and the Holy

Spirit, and to faith, love and hope. The standard ideas so characteristic of Christianity were already in place.

- *This is a short letter. You will have time to read it more than once, and to reflect upon its message.*
- *Paul's description of the second coming echoes the language to be attributed to Jesus in the Gospels (for example Mk 13:3–37, even the admonition to stay awake!). That Jesus will come again in glory to judge the living and the dead is part of our Creed. How important to us, in the twenty-first century, is this expectation?*

Chapter 7
Galatians

Who were the Galatians? Strictly, they were a people who inhabited what is now central Turkey, but in about 25 BCE Rome had incorporated them into a larger province of Galatia, which extended south towards the Mediterranean and included the cities of Antioch in Pisidia, Iconium, Lystra and Derbe, which Paul had evangelised on his first missionary journey (Acts 13:13, 51; 14:1–7).

- See maps on pages 33 and 41.

Paul's letter is addressed to 'the churches of Galatia' (1:2) and he addresses his readers in 3:1 simply as 'Galatians'. A great deal of scholarly effort has been expended on trying to identify whether that meant only the people to the north, or also the people in the southern cities mentioned in Acts. In truth, it does not matter. Paul's message comes through in either event.

Although Paul and Barnabas usually began their mission in the synagogues, many gentiles were converted, and it is obvious that it is mainly to them that this letter is addressed.

When Paul and Barnabas returned to Antioch (Acts 14:26) the problem arose that was to cause so much dissension in the early Church. Peter had already had the insight that salvation was offered not only to the Jews, but also to gentiles (Acts 10, 11:1–18). But many of the Jewish converts were so accustomed to the faith of their ancestors that they considered that, in order to be saved, gentiles would first have to become Jews, to be circumcised, and to live according to the Mosaic Law.

As recorded by Luke in Acts 15, some of these people, whom I will refer to as 'Judaisers', came to Antioch to preach this message.

> Judaisers is predominantly a Christian term derived from the Greek verb 'to live according to Jewish customs'. One of the customs of those Jews who lived according to the Law was that they would never eat in the company of uncircumcised gentiles

It is difficult to reconcile Paul's version of what happened next with Luke's account in Acts, so far as the timing is concerned. One hypothesis is that Luke has combined two meetings at Jerusalem into one, as he may well have done in his stylised account. At the first, Peter agreed with Paul (Acts 15:7-12), and Paul returned to Antioch. The issue about circumcision had been settled. At the second, Peter and Paul were not present, and James, the leader of the church in Jerusalem, spoke and put forward a solution to a different problem, namely the Jewish dietary laws, such as the prohibition on eating blood in Leviticus 17:10-14, (Acts 15:13-21), and this was what was set out in the letter that was sent to Antioch. The Simeon referred to by James at 15:14 was not Simon Peter, but Simeon Niger, the prophet and teacher from Antioch mentioned at Acts 13:1. The letter was delivered by Judas and Silas (Acts 15:27-32). Paul found out about the letter later (Acts 21:25), after his second mission.

> Note: See the article 'Paul', by Joseph A Fitzmyer in *The New Jerome biblical commentary* at 79:31-36.

However, be that as it may, this is a problem that should not concern us greatly at this stage. What is clear is that the decision was made that it was not necessary for gentiles to be circumcised in order to be saved, and that Paul and Barnabas were able to take that message back to Antioch. Paul had prevailed in that battle, but the war had not yet been won.

It appears from Gal 2:11-14 that Peter later visited Antioch. At first he was happy to act in accordance with the doctrine that he had proclaimed at Jerusalem, and to eat with everyone, circumcised or not. One of the reasons why this particular rule was so contentious was that it affected the community in their worship. Paul could see that it struck at the heart of the oneness in Christ of all believers if there were to be in the one Church two separate eucharists, one for the circumcised and one for gentiles. At Antioch this mattered, because it was a community of Jewish and gentile converts.

Then the Judaisers appeared again, and brought pressure to bear, no doubt claiming to have authority from James, the conservative head of the Church in Jerusalem. Peter may well have thought that he was being diplomatic, and began to eat separately.

Paul confronted him. Paul's letter is not an unbiased account, but even he does not suggest that, when confronted, Peter agreed with him. How it must have hurt Paul that even Barnabas was led astray. How isolated he must have felt when it seemed that pillars of the Church such as James, Barnabas and even Peter did not share his vision of the truth of the Gospel.

It is difficult to appreciate Paul's message in this letter without some idea of the strength of the message that the Judaisers were able to put. They would have agreed with Paul that faith in Christ had a role in the salvation of gentiles and Jews, but claimed that justification was not complete without observing the works of the Law, the great heritage of Judaism, with all its ethical guidance. Jesus himself had been an observant Jew. He had himself been circumcised, and had never purported to exempt anyone from circumcision. Part of the tradition about him, as would later be recorded by Matthew, was that he had not come to abolish the law but to fulfil it (Mt 5:17-19). The real apostles in Jerusalem kept the feasts and the food laws.

Paul could not be trusted to preach the whole of the true gospel, they would say. He could not really be called an apostle. He had never even met Jesus, as the real apostles had. When the apostles decided to replace Judas, they had chosen one who had been with them and Jesus from the baptism of John (Acts 1:21-26). They had not made any decision to add Paul to their number as an apostle. It is easy to understand that many might well have been persuaded by their arguments.

Now, we return shortly to the story in Acts.

Paul, in Antioch, decided to revisit the churches he had founded on his first journey with Barnabas, but this time there was a disagreement between them, which, in the light of recent events, may not have been entirely due to John Mark (Acts 15:36-41). He set out with Silas through Syria and Cilicia, and on to Galatia, where they went from town to town, delivering the decisions that had been reached by the apostles and elders in Jerusalem (16:1-4). It was in Lystra that Timothy joined Paul and Silas.

Why on earth did he have Timothy circumcised (16:3) when he was so insistent that circumcision was not necessary for salvation? It was because Timothy was in fact Jewish, because his mother was Jewish. Paul did not have any issue with Jews being circumcised, and, if asked, he would have proclaimed himself to be a Jewish Christian. His message was that gentiles did not have to become Jews in order to be saved.

Timothy had a Greek father, and a Greek name, but a Jewish mother. Paul wanted Timothy to accompany him on his mission. He would be going into Jewish synagogues. It would only cause trouble if he took with him a young man who, though Jewish, was not circumcised. It would also send the wrong message about what his teaching really was, and provide ammunition to his enemies in the Jewish community, who would say he was attacking Judaism itself, when he was not.

Then, as we know, he received the call to cross over to Macedonia (Acts 16:6-12). After his travels in Greece, he returned from Corinth to Jerusalem, and, after another visit to Antioch and Galatia (Acts 18:22-23), returned to Ephesus (Acts 19:1), where he remained for more than two years (Acts 19:8-10).

It is likely that while he was in Ephesus news came to him that the Judaisers were again active in Galatia, and obviously were having some success, and it was from Ephesus that he wrote this letter, in about 54 or 55 CE.

It is a very emotional letter. Paul is angry with the Judaisers and, perhaps even more, bewildered that his Galatians have been led astray by them. When he had first come among them he had been ill, but instead of despising him they had greeted him 'as an angel of God, as Christ Jesus'. They would have torn out their eyes for him (4:13-15). God had worked miracles among them while he had been with them (3:5). He is perplexed. He is 'in the pain of childbirth until Christ is formed in you' (4:19). He is so upset that in his introduction he omits his customary thanksgiving, and expresses astonishment that they are turning aside from the true gospel.

Paul's main thesis is that the gospel that he had preached to them came from a direct divine revelation to him, and not from human beings. From the very first line he attacks the suggestion that he is not a true apostle. He outlines his own conversion, his independence from the leaders in Jerusalem, his confrontation with the Judaisers there, and the acknowledgement by those leaders that he had been entrusted with the gospel (1:11—2:10).

In opposition to the case being put by the Judaisers he firmly states his own case–we are justified, that is, we are placed in a right relationship with God, not by doing the works prescribed by the law, but by faith in Jesus Christ (2:15-21). He then backs up his case with six arguments.

From experience (3:1-5). The Galatians had received the Spirit and seen miracles, without having observed the law, so the works of the law are obviously not necessary.

From Scripture (3:6-14). Paul quotes Genesis 12:3, where God promised Abraham that all nations would be blessed in him, a promise independent of circumcision. Abraham was justified by believing, before the covenant of circumcision had been entered into (Genesis 15:6, 17-20). God is keeping his promise to Abraham by giving the Spirit to the uncircumcised through faith.

By analogy (3:15-29). Just as a will that has been ratified cannot be annulled by a later addition, so the promises made to Abraham cannot be made dependent on the Mosaic Law, which came long after the promise. The law was only temporary until Christ should come.

Another analogy with some overlap with the previous argument (3:23—4:11). Until Christ came, although we were heirs to the promise we were like little children, no better than slaves. Now that Christ has come, why would the Galatians want to be enslaved again?

Friendship (4:12-20). The Galatians had been so kind to him while he had been with them. How could they possibly now treat him like an enemy?

An allegory based on scripture (4:21—5:1). This type of argument, interpreting Scripture freely, not literally, and in such a way as to reveal a hidden meaning, appears strange and unconvincing to us, though both Paul and his enemies were quite at home with it. Apparently the Judaisers had drawn some lesson from the story in Genesis about Abraham, who had two sons, the first, Ishmael, by his wife's slave girl, Hagar (Genesis 16) and the second, Isaac, by his wife Sarah (Genesis

21). According to the Hebrew text that has come down to us, Sarah became jealous when she saw Ishmael playing with Isaac. Paul either freely interpreted her reaction to the playing as persecution, or he was relying on some text that we do not have. However, Sarah asked Abraham to get rid of the slave girl and her son, so that Ishmael should not inherit along with Isaac and God approved of his doing so (Gen 21:9–20).

We are not told what allegory his opponents drew from all this, but Paul's response is, 'That's not an allegory, this is an allegory.' He produces his own interpretation. Hagar, the slave girl, represents the earthly Jerusalem, subject to the Mosaic covenant given at Mount Sinai and enslaved to the law with her children. The other woman, Sarah, corresponds to the heavenly Jerusalem, and she is free. His Galatians are children of the promise made to Abraham, and are free. With some irony (4:21), Paul suggests that the Galatians should follow the story in Genesis (part of the Torah, the source of the Law), cast out the Judaisers and never again submit to slavery.

Paul passionately sets out three practical consequences of his arguments:

(5:1–12) His readers should preserve the freedom that they have in Christ. Verse 11 is a response by Paul to suggestions by his opponents that he admitted the validity of circumcision when it suited him. He had, after all, had Timothy circumcised (Acts 16:3). He answers that if he were still preaching circumcision why would they still be opposing him? The bitterness of his anger blazes out in verse 12.

(5:13–26) They should live by the Spirit and not by the flesh. The Spirit expresses itself in love of one another, the flesh in self-indulgence.

(6:1–10) They should obey the Spirit by helping one another.

Paul then takes the pen from the scribe and writes his own conclusion to the letter (6:11–18). His opponents may want to boast about making converts. He boasts only of the cross. In the new creation of Christ, circumcision does not matter. What he has suffered as an apostle is more important than his circumcision. He ends with his usual invocation that the grace of Christ be with his beloved Galatians.

- *Unlike Paul's Galatians, we are not in danger of being led astray to believe that we must obey the ritual practices of the Mosaic law in order to be saved. What lessons are there for us in this letter?*

Chapter 8
Philippians and Philemon

It is clear from the internal evidence that Paul wrote both these letters while he was in prison. When and where was that? We cannot be certain, and many scholars have written a great deal about the place and time. Luke, in Acts, tells of only two occasions when Paul was in prison for any extended period:
- when he was taken into protective custody by the Romans in Jerusalem and removed to Caesarea
- after appealing to Caesar, he was taken to Rome.

However, both these locations are difficult to reconcile with the frequent contacts between Paul and the Philippians that are mentioned in the letter, because of the great distances involved.

Luke does not tell of any imprisonment in Ephesus, but Paul was there for two to three years (Acts 19:1, 8–10, 20:23), and in 2 Corinthians, written before he was imprisoned in Caesarea or Rome, he speaks of being in peril in Asia (2 Cor 1:8–11) and of having been imprisoned many times (2 Cor 6:5, 11:23). The references in Phil 1:13 to the Imperial Guard and in Phil 4:22 to the 'Emperor's household' do not show that he was writing from Rome. The phrase 'Emperor's household' covered those involved in imperial administration. A modern equivalent might be 'public servants'. Inscriptions record their presence in Ephesus. On balance the best arguments appear to favour Ephesus, which would date Philippians to about 54–56 CE.

The letter to Philemon contains even fewer clues than Philippians. In this case there is no difficulty in attributing it either to Ephesus or Rome. The weight of opinion favours Ephesus, at about the same time as Philippians. But if, as will be discussed later, Paul was the author of

Colossians, then he may well have sent this letter from Rome, about 60 CE.

There has also been a great deal of discussion about whether Philippians is one letter, or an edited version that combines parts of two or even three letters. This issue also is one that need not concern us greatly. Both letters are undoubtedly from Paul, and reveal a great deal about the beauty of his character.

The letter to the Philippians

> Review Acts 16:11–40

When Paul, Timothy and perhaps Luke crossed over to Macedonia, the first city in which they stayed was Philippi—Neapolis was its port, about ten miles away (see map on page 27). Philippi was a major Roman city, where veterans from the Roman army had been settled for over a century, and it was administered under the same Roman law that applied in Italy. This explains the reaction of the magistrates when they discovered that Paul was a Roman citizen.

The Jewish community met and prayed by a stream outside the walls, and there Lydia was converted, together with her household. She was not Jewish, but a 'worshipper of God', and, as a dealer in purple cloth, a rich woman—purple cloth was claimed to be worth its weight in silver. She was also, obviously, a forceful character, because Paul usually liked to preserve his independence. There is a lot implied in Luke's 'she prevailed upon us'.

I do not read, 'we remained in this city for some days', as describing the total length of their stay in Philippi. I think Luke means that it was after only a few days that they went to the place of prayer on the Sabbath. It is quite obvious from the letter that Paul formed a very close and fruitful relationship with the people there. They were to support his mission financially on a number of occasions. Many of the community were probably gentile converts, and it would seem that some women were prominent.

> Note: The letter to the Philippians is short, and it would be beneficial to read all of it once to get a general impression, and then to read it again more carefully.

In the opening formula (1:1-2) Paul refers to his readers as 'the saints in Jesus Christ'. They make up in Christ God's holy people. The reference to bishops and deacons does not mean that the church was already organised into the offices that appeared later. The words were used in secular language to mean simply overseers and ministers or helpers, and both descriptions could apply to the one person.

Then follows Paul's beautiful prayer of thanksgiving (1:3-11) and his reflections upon his imprisonment (1:12-26). His exhortations to the community follow (1:27—2:18). He calls them to unity and selflessness among themselves, and steadfastness in the face of persecution.

Verses 2:6-11 in the original Greek are in poetic form, and scholars suggest that Paul may well have been quoting a hymn that was already in use in the community. His Philippians should follow the example of Christ, who showed that the way to God was not by exploiting a high position for one's own advantage, but by being humbly obedient to the Father's will. Paul tells them that he is sending Epaphroditus to them immediately, and promises to send Timothy soon after (2:19-30).

It seems that the Judaisers were troubling this community, as they had the Galatians. This time, however, Paul's anger is directed at them, rather than at his readers (3:2-4:1). It is remarkable how much of his own spirituality he reveals, centred as always on Christ, not on compliance with the precepts of the Law.

The body of the letter concludes with further exhortations, first for unity between two women who had worked hard beside him for the sake of the Gospel. He urges his readers to rejoice, as he rejoices in gratitude for all they had done for him. He ends with a farewell and his usual final blessing.

The Letter to Philemon

This carefully crafted and polished gem is Paul's shortest letter. Some have questioned why a personal letter to a friend, not to a church, should have been preserved and treasured by the universal Church. Yet not far below the surface lies some important Pauline theology. It also illustrates what a master of the psychology of persuasion Paul was.

In addition, although Paul makes no attack upon the institution of slavery, the basis of his appeal to Philemon, that he should receive Onesimus back as a brother in Christ, transcends that institution, and provides the true basis for its abolition. Brown comments, 'in every line just beneath the surface is the basic challenge to the societal rank of master and slave offered by the changed relationship introduced by the Gospel.' Why did it take society 1700 years to realise that truth?

It would seem that Philemon was a relatively rich Christian. His house was big enough to be the meeting place for the Christian community, and he had at least one slave. Apphia may have been his wife and Archippus a member of his household, or someone prominent in the local church. Philemon probably owed his conversion to Paul (v 19).

Onesimus was Philemon's slave, who had run away, perhaps after causing some loss to his master (vv 11, 18–19). Verse 11 is a pun on his name, as Onesimus meant 'profitable one'. We are not told how he encountered Paul. He had obviously become not only his convert, but a very close friend and helper to Paul in prison.

Paul deliberately does not use his position as an apostle to get what he wants. He begins his letter by describing himself as a prisoner, and bases his appeal on love (vv 1, 8, 9).

The punishments permitted for a runaway slave were brutally severe. Paul does not ask merely that Philemon refrain from punishment and accept from Paul compensation for any loss Onesimus might have caused, which would have been noble enough. He asks that the relationship between Philemon and Onesimus be raised to a completely different plane—'receive him as you would receive me' (v 17), followed by 'I say nothing about your owing me even your own self' (v 19).

How could Philemon refuse? The fact that the letter survived and was treasured demonstrates that Paul's advocacy was effective.

- *As you read this letter, ask yourself not only, 'What do I think?' but also, 'How do I feel? How must Philemon have felt?'*

Chapter 9
1 Corinthians

In Acts 17:16–34 we read about Paul, on his second missionary journey, waiting for Timothy and Silas in Athens, the cultural centre of the Greco-Roman world. There he addressed the philosophers in their own language, in a speech which, as Luke records it, was a polished gem of rhetoric. Yet we have no letter to the Athenians. Why not? It was because Paul did not succeed in founding a community there. There were a few converts, but in general he was received with politeness at best and ridicule at worst. He left Athens and travelled the short distance of about eighty km (fifty miles) to Corinth.

The part of Greece known as Achaia is almost an island, joined to the mainland by a narrow isthmus, only about four miles wide. On a plateau at the southern end of the isthmus, with a high fortified hill behind it, was the city of Corinth. Obviously it was in a position to profit from traffic between Achaia and the mainland, but it also provided a desirable and sheltered shortcut for shipping traveling between Athens and the Aegean Sea to the east and the Adriatic Sea and the coast of the mainland to the West. A 1.5 m (five foot) wide track had been cut in the rock to enable small vessels and their cargo to be moved overland from one port to the other.

See maps pages 33 and 41.

Fig. 9.1
Some ruins of ancient Corinth with the acropolis in the background.

The city had been destroyed by the Romans in 146 BCE but it was restored by Julius Caesar in 44 BCE and settled by freed men from Italy, Greece, Syria, Egypt and Judea. By Paul's time it was much larger and richer than Athens, and was the capital of the province, ruled by a proconsul sent from Rome. In 51-52 CE the proconsul was Gallio, who dismissed the complaint brought against Paul by his Jewish enemies as recounted in Acts 18:12-17.

The community to which Paul was writing was diverse. There were Jews and many pagan converts, from all ranks of society, except perhaps the very top and very bottom of the Greco-Roman social scale. The names of sixteen people whom he met there are known, from Acts 18, 1 Corinthians 16 and Romans 16, but the most important are his trusted fellow workers Aquila and his wife Priscilla. He spent a year and a half with the Corinthians (Acts 18:11) and then set out to return to Antioch, by way of Ephesus, Caesarea and Jerusalem. He took Priscilla and Aquila with him as far as Ephesus, but left them there to guide the local church (Acts 18:18-22).

Paul himself tells us that he wrote this letter while in Ephesus (16:8), most probably in the spring of 54 CE but possibly a year or two later. He had already written one letter to them (5:9), which has not survived, warning them about associating with immoral Christians.

The Corinthians had also written to him, raising a number of problems on which they wanted his advice (7:1). Stephanas, Fortunatus and Achaicus, mentioned in 16:17, may have brought the letter. In addition, some representatives of a woman named Chloe, of whom we know nothing, had come to Ephesus from Corinth, and reported to Paul some disturbing aspects of the church there, particularly the rise of factions amongst the Christians (1:11-12).

Structure of the letter

The letter begins with his usual greeting and thanksgiving.

In the first part of the body of his letter Paul deals directly with the problems of divisions in the community (1:10—4:21). They were claiming to belong to various factions, purporting to follow various teachers such as Paul himself, Apollos or Cephas.

Apollos was a Jewish convert from Alexandria, who had come to Ephesus and preached the gospel there with eloquence, while himself learning more about it from Priscilla and Aquila. He had then gone to Corinth while Paul was on his way from there to Ephesus (Acts 18:24—19:1). He was in Ephesus with Paul when this letter was being written, and Paul was obviously on good terms with him (16:12). Cephas, of course, was Peter.

Paul rapidly demonstrates the futility of factions, including especially those who might claim to follow him (1:13). He emphasises the centrality of belief in Jesus crucified and risen, a belief that is foolishness to the wise of this world, and a stumbling block to the Jews. God's wisdom is different. It is obvious that Paul is still affected by the failure of his mission to the philosophers in Athens, whom he had addressed with worldly eloquence, and his negative reception by the Jewish community at large in Corinth (Acts 18:5-7). Paul appeals to his Corinthians to imitate him, and has sent Timothy to them to remind them of his teaching. He hopes to come to them himself, if the Lord wills, and to deal with any who do not get the message (4:18-21).

In the second part he deals with two misunderstandings that seem to have become widespread in the Corinthian community (5:1—6:20). He had taught them, of course, about the freedom from the slavery of sin that comes with faith in Jesus, but some had reduced his teaching to mere slogans, such as 'all things are lawful for me' (6:12). They had come to believe perhaps that physical actions have no spiritual significance. Paul had written to them earlier about associating with sexually immoral persons, in a letter that has been lost to us. He points out that sexual immorality defiles the church and should be cast out.

At first sight sexual immorality and lawsuits may seem unrelated, but to Paul they are both an affront to the unity of believers in the one body of Christ about which he is to write so eloquently later in this letter (12:12-27).

In the third part of his letter Paul addresses a series of questions about which the Corinthians had written to him (7:1—14:40). They may conveniently be grouped as:
- problems of social status (7:1-40)
- problems arising from their pagan environment (8:1—11:1), and
- problems in liturgical assemblies (11:2—14:40).

When we read the section about marriage and virginity (7:1–40), we should bear in mind that Paul is writing less than twenty-five years after the Ascension, when the second coming of Christ was expected in the near future. He speaks of 'the impending crisis' (7:26), 'the appointed time has grown short' (7:29) and 'For the present form of this world is passing away' (7:31).

Part of the liturgy of paganism (and indeed of Judaism) was that the worshippers took part by eating the food that had been offered to the god. Some converts took the view that, since the gods worshipped by the idolaters simply did not exist, there was no harm in eating such food. Many others, after their long association with paganism before their conversion, worried that eating such foods could seem to give credence to idolatry. They have asked Paul for his advice. Paul acknowledges the truth in the slogans of the former, such as, 'no idol in the world really exists', but admonishes them, since the impact of one's actions on others should guide a Christian's decision. He illustrates his point by showing that in his own life he has accepted limitations on his own freedom for the good of others. Again he limits the force of their slogan, 'all things are lawful', and ends this section with some sensible, practical advice.

The next two topics may not have been raised by Paul in answer to questions in the letter to him, but seem more to arise out of what he had been told by Chloe's people. Perhaps in the letter, after asking about idol meats, they had written something to the effect that they were following the traditions he had left them, such as coming together to celebrate the Eucharist. In their newfound freedom, however, some of their behaviours called for criticism.

First, the head coverings of some men and women at their liturgical gatherings were not appropriate, in the light of the customs of the time (11:4–16). Paul is not setting up some hierarchy of men over women —both come from God (11:12)— but is referring back to the story of creation in Gen 2. Men and women are different, and should dress accordingly.

Next, he deals with some abuses that had arisen in connection with their eucharistic gatherings (11:17–34). His essential message is that the Eucharist should be an occasion for unity in Christ and having concern for each other, not distinctions between rich and poor. Paul's version of the words of institution (11:23–25) is closest to that of Luke

(Lk 22:15-20), but of course much earlier. He bases his version, not on tradition, but on direct revelation from the Lord (11:23).

He then returns to a question raised by the Corinthians, a supposed hierarchy of spiritual gifts (12:1—14:40). His point is that there is no hierarchy and there should be no competitiveness or pride. All the gifts are allotted by the Spirit as the Spirit chooses (12:11), for the benefit of the whole community. Chapter 13 comprises Paul's immortal hymn in praise of Love. In that context chapter 14 gives practical guidance to ensure that the gifts are used for the good of all (14:26).

There is general agreement among scholars now that verses 14:34-36, about women being silent in church and subordinate to their husbands, were not written by Paul, but were inserted by a later author. They are inconsistent with what Paul had written in 11:5.

It is not clear just how it had come to Paul's notice that some of the Corinthians were saying that there was no resurrection of the dead or on what basis they held that belief. Possibly some believed that they already had eternal life, and attached no importance to the body. Paul's response is based on the belief of the church in the resurrection of Christ. He points out the inevitable consequences of their denial of Christ's resurrection and benefits of his affirmation (15:1-58). It seems that Paul still expected Christ's second coming to happen within his own lifetime (15:51-53).

> It was Paul who first used the term 'gospel', (*evangélion*, Greek for 'the good message') when he reminded the people 'of the gospel I preached to you' (15:1).

Paul expected the Corinthians to contribute to the collection for the benefit of the poor in Jerusalem about which he had spoken in Galatians 2:10. His practical advice acknowledges that they could put together a respectable contribution only if they put aside a little each week (16:1-4).

After discussing his plans to travel to visit them, and commending the work of a number of his fellow workers to them, Paul concludes with his customary blessing.

Chapter 10
2 Corinthians

Paul had a long and complex relationship with the community that he founded at Corinth. We need some effort of the imagination to appreciate the difficulties that he had with them. Remember, the time is less than thirty years since the resurrection. Neither they nor Paul had the advantages that we have from many centuries of reflection and analysis by saints and scholars on what the Christ event meant for Christian living.

The majority were converts from paganism, from nearly all ranks of society, and they lived in a society that was still thoroughly pagan, unlike ours, which stands at the end of many centuries of Christian civilisation. Corinth had a reputation for sexual licence, probably worse than it deserved, but in any event it was a rough, multicultural, relatively new city with two seaports and a booming economy.

Scholars have also had great difficulty in deducing the chronology of Paul's dealings with the Corinthians from the clues in the letters. There is considerable disagreement, and there can be no certainty, but the summary given by Brown is credible and sufficient for our purposes (*Introduction to the New Testament*, 514–515, 541–544).

In 51–52 CE Paul was in Corinth, having arrived there from Athens. He left, with Priscilla and Aquila, and by 56 CE was in Ephesus.

Other missionaries such as Apollos carried on the work in Corinth, as we have seen. Paul wrote them a letter, now lost, telling them not to have dealings with immoral people (1 Cor 5:9). At Ephesus, he received reports from Chloe's people, and a letter from the Corinthians, which led to his writing 1 Corinthians.

Early in 57 CE Timothy arrived in Corinth, having been sent there by Paul (1 Cor 4:17-19). He was disturbed by what he found, including false apostles hostile to Paul (2 Cor 11:12-15). He returned to Ephesus and reported to Paul.

Paul set out to Corinth, probably by sea. His visit was a painful one (2 Cor 2:1). He felt that he was perceived as ineffectual when face to face with them (2 Cor 10:1; 10), and that his authority was challenged (2 Cor 2:5-11; 7:12). He left, planning to return quickly, but changed his mind, realising that it would only be another painful visit (2 Cor 2:1).

Instead, he wrote another letter, 'with many tears' (2 Cor 2:3-4; 7:8-9). It was taken to Corinth by Titus. That letter also has been lost.

Titus was well received at Corinth (7:13-15), and he was able to collect money for Paul to take to Jerusalem (8:6).

Meanwhile Paul had returned to Macedonia, where Titus eventually met him and was able to report on the repentance of the Corinthians (2 Cor 7:5-13). With Timothy at his side, Paul immediately responded with the letter we know as 2 Corinthians. Its date was not long after 1 Corinthians perhaps in about 57 CE.

We have by now read enough of Paul to realise that he does not always develop his thoughts in a strictly logical sequence or without complications. Brown comments that, 'perhaps no other letter of Paul evokes so vividly the image of a suffering and rejected apostle, misunderstood by his fellow Christians' (ibid. 541).

Some scholars have argued that the transitions from one part of the letter to another are so abrupt that 2 Corinthians must be a composite of a number of separate letters, perhaps even as many as five. Most agree that 6:14-7:1 is a passage inserted by a later editor.

> Note: Read how smoothly the theme of open hearts in 6:13 is picked up in 7:2). But there is no doubt that all the rest was written by Paul.

There is indeed a noticeable change in tone from the celebration of reconciliation in chapters 1-9 to the reproaches and self-vindication in chapters 10-13. However, as Brown comments, for us to 'understand what Paul wants to communicate it will suffice to recognise that 2 Corinthians contains different topics expressed with different rhetorical emphases' (ibid 551).

After the opening formula (1:1-2) and thanksgiving (1:3-11), part one of the body of the letter discusses Paul's dealings with the Corinthians, not simply as history, but from his theological viewpoint (1:12—7:16).

Part two (8:1—9:15) deals with his collection for the church in Jerusalem.

In part three (10:1—13:10) Paul responds to the challenges to his apostolic authority. His many references to being a fool reflect a common convention of theatrical productions of his time, in which a recognisable conventional character, 'the fool' was able to highlight the faults and failings of other characters in the play.

His final exhortation to them is in the concluding formula (13:11-13). Reflect upon the beauty of his final blessing, which is the source of a common liturgical blessing used in our church today—Grace from Jesus Christ, love from God, and communion, or fellowship, from the Holy Spirit.

Chapter 11
Romans

As he had promised in 2 Corinthians 13:1, Paul visited Corinth a third time, probably about 57/58 CE. Perhaps this visit was successful, and he felt that his work was done in the East. He had long wished to carry the Gospel to the far west of the Roman empire, to Spain, and to visit Rome on the way, but first he had to take to Jerusalem the collection from the Greek churches (Rom 1:9-15; 15:20-29). He wrote this letter, probably from Corinth, perhaps from Cenchrae, its eastern port, where he was the guest of Gaius (Rom 16:23), whom he had baptised on his first visit to Corinth (1 Cor 1:14). He commends to the Romans his friend and benefactor Phoebe, a deacon from Cenchrae (Rom 16:1-3), who may well have carried the letter to Rome. As Luke recounts in Acts, he then travelled through Greece, Asia Minor and Caesarea to Jerusalem, where he was arrested (Acts 22:22—24:27). He was indeed to come to the Romans, not on his way to Spain (Rom 15:24), but as a prisoner.

There were many Jews in Rome in the first century, and it would have been natural for some Jewish converts to make their way there as missionaries. The original community was probably conservative about their Jewish heritage and the Law. In 49 CE the emperor Claudius had expelled Jews and Jewish Christians from Rome. Luke attributes the presence of Aquila and Priscilla in Corinth to this event (Acts18:2). That would have left gentile converts to develop independently of Jewish Christian influence, so that regulations about dietary and calendar matters did not matter so much to them. There is no evidence that Peter had arrived in Rome at the time of Paul's letter.

> Suetonius writing in 121 CE suggests that constant disturbances in the Jewish community led to their expulsion. Suetonius viewed Christians as 'a class of men given to a new and mischievous superstition', and his contemporary Tacitus suggested that 'this pernicious superstition' had originated in Judea.

After the death of Claudius in 54 CE, Nero lifted the ban, allowing Jewish Christians to return to Rome. They included Aquila and Priscilla, so that Paul is able to include a commendation of them in his letter (Rom 16:3-4). The long list of friends in chapter 16 indicates a substantial community in which Paul already had many contacts. The date of the letter was most probably in 57 or 58 CE.

The community to which he was writing, therefore, included both Jewish and gentile converts, and the relationship of Christianity to Judaism would still have been a most important topic of concern, which Paul addresses in this letter.

We must remember that none of the gospels had yet been written. There possibly existed some collections of sayings of the Lord, but the only extant writings reflecting on the significance of the Christ event were his own previous letters. Paul does not attempt to set out a systematic and complete statement of his theology. His basic theme is the possibility of salvation, now offered to all human beings, not through deeds prescribed by the Law of Moses, but through faith in Jesus Christ.

A number of the topics that he deals with in this letter are similar to those in Galatians, but the crisis that had led to his anger in that letter had now passed. There is no suggestion that there were adversaries in Rome preaching the necessity of circumcision or contesting his apostleship. Paul is able more peacefully to set out the results of his reflections on those problems over a number of years.

This is his longest letter, and undoubtedly his most important. Its influence on subsequent theology has been profound. It covers a number of important topics. It is not the easiest of his letters to comprehend. We need therefore to keep in mind the purpose of this project, namely to experience the whole of the New Testament, as a first step towards understanding it more fully later on.

This letter is one to which you will return many times. Do not be disheartened by difficulties. Make a note of them for later investigation and move on.

Paul was not writing to a community that he had founded, so he introduces himself at some length, attributing to Jesus Christ his call to be an apostle to the gentiles. After his customary prayer for God's grace and peace for them, he expresses his eagerness to share with them the riches of the Gospel (1:9–15).

After this introduction, the main body of the letter may be divided into three parts, doctrinal, hortatory and conclusion, with each of those parts having further subdivisions.

Doctrinal

In part one of the doctrinal section (1:16—4:25), Paul stresses that the righteousness of God is revealed through the gospel, which has power to save every believer, first the Jew, then the Greek. The pagans could have discovered God through creation, but their failure to do so had led to perversions of the natural order. But Jews are also condemned who profess to abhor what Paul has just condemned, but then do the same things. Circumcision may have had value for those who obeyed the law, but now there is no distinction. No one has the right to boast. All, Jews and Greeks, are justified by faith in Jesus. As in Galatians he cites the example of Abraham, father of all, who was justified by faith in God before the covenant of circumcision had been given.

In the next part (5:1—8:39), Paul sets out his sublime vision of our reconciliation to God in Christ, and the benefits that flow to us from that reconciliation, namely peace, hope and love through the Holy Spirit. He compares the grace and life that we receive through Christ with the sin and death that came to us through Adam. This death to sin and raising to life in Christ is what we receive at baptism.

He then addresses the Jewish converts, 'those who know the Law'. Although the law is not itself sin, our inevitable failure to be able to comply completely with it, because of our human weakness, gives rise to sin. Paul's basic principle is that Christ's death has annulled the binding power of the law. We are to live, not according to the flesh, but according to the Spirit, who bears witness that when we address God as 'father', we are children and heirs of God. We should not live in fear, but in hope, for even in our weakness the spirit intercedes for us. The passage with which Paul concludes this part of the doctrinal section (8:18–39) is rightly described as one of the most eloquent statements in all Christian writing.

In the third part of this doctrinal section, (9:1—11:36), Paul addresses what must have been a widespread concern in a Christian community that comprised both Jewish and gentile converts. How can the promises that God had made to Israel be reconciled with justification through faith in Christ, especially since it was by now obvious that official Judaism had rejected Christ?

We are accustomed to reading the Scriptures in discrete sections, separated into chapters that were devised centuries after the works were written. In Paul's letter there was no break between the sublimity of 8:31–39 and the astonishing expression of his anguish in 9:1–3. It is in the context of his declaration that nothing can separate us from the love of God in Christ that he proclaims himself willing to be cut off from Christ if only that could help reconcile his fellow Jews to Christ! In rebuttal of those who might suggest that he denigrated Judaism, whether in his time or in later centuries, he lists with pride the blessings given by God to his people, culminating in the Messiah (9:4–5).

This is a difficult problem. The Catholic Church has continued to struggle with it through the centuries, most recently at Vatican II, in *Nostra Aetate*. Paul had no precedents to guide him, and his answer does not solve all the problems. He bases his argument that God has not broken his promises on a number of biblical references. God's word has not failed. The children of the promise to Abraham included other than his descendants 'according to the flesh', and not all of those who were children of Israel according to the flesh were truly Israelites. God can have mercy on whom he chooses. He does not need to account to us for his actions (9:6–29). Israel's failure to attain righteousness arises from its own insistence on striving for it on the basis of works, not faith (9:30—10:21). But that failure of Israel is only partial and temporary. Not all Israelites have failed. Some have, like branches broken off an olive tree, and gentiles have been like wild branches grafted on to the tree, to share the riches of its roots. God can graft back onto the tree those Israelites who believe.

Both gentiles and Jews have been disobedient, but God shows mercy to all (11:1-36)

Hortatory

In the hortatory section Paul appeals to the Roman community, setting out how they should live in response to God's mercy.

In the first part (12:1—13:14) he recalls the imagery that he used in 1 Cor, that we are all members of the one body that is Christ. He exhorts them to be good citizens, while not being conformed to worldly standards of self-interest. [Claudius, who had expelled Jews from Rome, was dead, and the new emperor, Nero, had not yet displayed any hostility to Christians.]

In the second part (14:1—15:13) he seems to be alluding to differing practices about food and feast day observances, such as might be expected in such a mixed community. Just who were the 'strong' and who the 'weak' is not clear, but Paul's main concern is that neither group should judge or denigrate the other.

Conclusion

Paul begins the conclusion to his letter with an explanation of his plans and reasons for visiting, after he has delivered the funds collected for the faithful in Jerusalem (15:14-33). Since he has not yet been to Rome, he needs as many people as possible to put in a good word for him. He names twenty-six friends, but we know nothing about most of them apart from his descriptions in this letter. The passage indicates that the Roman community consisted of a number of small house churches.

Paul ends the letter with greetings from his co-workers at Corinth, and the scribe, Tertius, cannot refrain from including himself. The final doxology (16:25-27) is missing from many manuscripts and may be a later liturgical addition for public reading in church.

Chapter 12
Paul's attitude to women

Now that we have read all the letters that are acknowledged by scholars to be genuine Pauline letters, it is appropriate to consider the question of his attitude to women. There is a widespread view that he was a misogynist, that he had a low opinion of women, and taught that they should be kept in their place as subordinate to men. In fact, if Paul had heard the accusation he would have been astonished. The criticism that he would have expected would have been that he allowed to women far more status and freedom than society at that time thought proper.

The principal cause of the misunderstanding is that the evidence for his low opinion of women comes from letters, or parts of a letter, that he did not himself write. An example is, 'Let a woman learn in silence with full submission. I permit no woman to teach or to have authority over a man. She is to keep silent' (1 Tim 2:11). The passage is a part of scripture, and its meaning and application must be determined accordingly, but it was not Paul who wrote it. It was written in his name decades after Paul had died.

> Note: See the section 'Did he write them all?' in Ch. 5—the letters of Paul.

Another example occurs in a letter that is authentically Pauline. At 1 Corinthians 14, vv 33b–36, it is written that women should be silent in Church, and should be subordinate. In my version of the bible (NRSV) the passage is enclosed in brackets. Modern scholarship assures us that the passage was not written by Paul in his original letter, but was inserted by a later editor. Notice how the text flows naturally from verse 33a to verse 37 if the passage is omitted. The passage appeals to the law, which is not typical of Paul. It is also contradicted by 1 Corinthians11:5, where Paul, although he insists that she should have her head covered when she does so, obviously contemplates a woman praying or prophesying publicly. One of his close female associates, Priscilla, felt free to explain the Way more accurately to Apollos together with her husband Aquila (Acts 18:26).

Some critics point to 1 Corinthians 7:1, where it is written, 'It is well for a man not to touch a woman'. What they fail to notice is that Paul is not setting out his teaching in that phrase, but quoting one of the slogans used by some of the Corinthians. Paul then proceeds to demolish it, insisting on the rights of both husband and wife to enjoy sex. As we have seen, he may well have been a married man.

In his letter to the Philippians, when asking for help for those women, he writes that they had 'struggled beside me in the work of the gospel' (Phil 4:3). That is hardly a description of silent submission.

At the end of this letter to the Romans he refers by name to twenty-six people, who he expects to prepare the way for him in Rome. Nine of them are women. The first is Phoebe, a deacon. She is described as a 'benefactor of many and of myself as well.' (Rom 16:1). The word literally means 'patroness'. That means a person of substance, and she may well have provided funds for Paul's journey to Jerusalem. He obviously expects her to have great influence in preparing the way for him in Rome.

Next is Prisca, called by the affectionate diminutive 'Priscilla' in Acts 18:2, 18, 26. In Acts 18:26 we read that it was Priscilla and her husband who explained The Way more accurately to Apollos. They had 'risked their necks' for him, and not only he, but all the gentile churches gave thanks for them (3:3,4).

'Mary' has worked very hard among the Romans (16:6). Junia, his relative, has been in prison with him. He is hardly putting her down when he describes her as an apostle, and one who was in Christ before he was! (16:7). The mother of Rufus 'has been a mother to me also' (16:13).

The difference between Paul's authentic statements and the quote from 1 Timothy 2:11 illustrates the fact that we must not interpret the New Testament literally on the basis of one quotation. The whole must be taken into account, and distinctions drawn between admonitions that are meant for a particular time and place according to the culture of the time, and the essential message of the Good News.

He summed it up himself, in his letter to the Galatians (3:28), 'There is no longer Jew or Greek, there is no longer slave or free, there is no longer male and female, for all of you are one in Christ Jesus'.

Chapter 13
1 Peter

1 Peter is the first of a group of seven New Testament documents—James, 1 and 2 Peter, 1, 2 and 3 John and Jude—that are called the 'Catholic' epistles. They are so named because they were not intended for a single community, as were Paul's letters, but were for a wider audience, or the whole Church.

This letter purports to have been written by the apostle Peter, and is addressed to 'the exiles of the diaspora in Pontus, Galatia, Cappadocia, Asia and Bithynia'. Those places encompass roughly the northern part of modern Turkey. The diaspora was a term that had been used to describe the body of Jews scattered after the Babylonian captivity 587 BCE, but it is apparent from the contents of the letter that it was addressed mainly to gentile Christians who were scattered throughout the Roman world.

It had been accepted from the time of Eusebius (3rd and 4th century) until the 19th century that the letter was indeed written by the head of the Apostles. The question is still disputed in modern scholarship. The style of the Greek original is not what one would expect from a Galilean fisherman, but that may be explained by the fact that it was almost certainly produced by a secretary, Silvanus (5:12), who would have had considerable freedom in the composition of a letter. There are other arguments for and against, with eminent scholars holding different views, but the problem is not one that we can or need solve at this stage.

The letter purports to have been written from the 'Church in Babylon', which was at that time code among Christians for Rome. Peter spent some time in Rome, and was executed there during Nero's persecution, in about 65 CE. If Peter indeed wrote the letter, it would be dated to shortly before that time.

If someone else was the author, it was most probably a disciple who was closely associated with the Petrine heritage and community in Rome, and who wrote not long after Peter's death, between 70 and 90 CE.

Two members of the community mentioned in the letter are Silvanus and Mark (5:12-13). In Acts 15:22, 27 Luke recounts that the apostles in Jerusalem had sent Silvanus (there called Silas), a leader among the brethren, to Antioch together with Paul, Barnabas and Judas to convey their letter following the meeting at Jerusalem. After his disagreement with Barnabas about taking Mark, Paul took Silvanus as his companion on his second missionary journey as far as Corinth.

Although it is not certain, it is quite possible that John Mark, whom Peter knew in Jerusalem (Acts 12:12), and who was a companion of Paul for a time, came to Rome and joined Peter there. For a time there was a theory, no longer widely held, that Mark's gospel was, in effect, the Good News according to Peter.

The letter is pastoral. The people to whom it is addressed are suffering various trials, especially misunderstanding by the pagans among whom they live. They are encouraged to remain faithful.

After the short introduction (1:1-2) the first part of the body of the letter speaks about the dignity of the Christian vocation and its responsibilities (1:3—2:10).

The second part (2:11—3:12) gives practical advice about giving witness by living the Christian life in a pagan world, especially by humility and love for each other.

The third part (3:13—5:11) deals with the Christian approach to persecution and misunderstanding, based on the example of Christ.

The letter concludes with an admonition to stand firm in the true grace of God, final greetings from the author, Silvanus and Mark, and a blessing of peace.

- *Does our situation in twenty-first century Australia bear any resemblance to that of the people to whom 1 Peter was written? Does the letter have any special lessons for us also?*

Chapter 14
How to read a gospel

Fig. 14.1
This beautiful illustration is from the *Codex Aureus of Lorsch* or Lorsch Gospels. It is an illuminated Gospel Book written between 778 and 820. It was first recorded in Lorsch Abbey (Germany). Each of the gospel chapters has an illustration from this book. You can see in glorious colour at Wikimedia Commons

> *Note:* In writing this introduction to the gospels and in the discussion of each one of them I am most indebted to the book *The living voice of the Gospels: the Gospels today* (2nd Ed. John Garratt Publishing 2006) by Francis J Moloney. It is beyond the scope of this work to summarise all the insights into the Gospels that Moloney makes so clear. Yet they are necessary for a proper understanding.

When we come to read all four gospels with a little care, we will notice that they are not a satisfactory historical account of the life of Jesus. There are too many differences between them.

For example, in Matthew, Mark and Luke, the public life of Jesus spans one year. There is only one Passover. In John it lasts three years and there are three Passovers. The version of the calling of the first apostles in Mark 1:16–20 is quite different from that in John 1:35–51. Matthew gives a summary of Jesus' teaching, including ten beatitudes, as a sermon on a mountain (Matt 5:1—7:28). Luke's version of the discourse is much shorter, with only three beatitudes, and Jesus delivers it on a level place after coming down from the mountain where he had been praying (Luke 6:12-49). The versions of what happened and when on the morning of the resurrection differ. There are many other such instances.

We must begin by accepting that the gospels are not history books, as we would understand history. Their authors did not intend to write factual histories, and the communities for whom the books were written did not read or listen to them as if they were.

On the other hand they are not mere literary inventions. They are based on real events that happened during and after the life, death and resurrection of Jesus Christ. In essence each gospel is an attempt by the author to set out aspects of the meaning of those events for humanity by telling stories about them. They are theological works. They were not written to convince unbelievers. They were addressed to believing communities in order to strengthen and enlighten their faith.

The gospels, in a way, are like portraits of the one person by four different artists. Each will have different colours, background, clothing and facial expression, but each will be instantly recognisable as a true portrait of the subject.

The evangelists were influenced by the literary sources to which they had access, by the communities in which the Jesus story had been preserved and developed, and by their own literary style and genius. The stories are chosen, recounted and arranged in such a way as to highlight diverse theological insights into the Christ event that the evangelist wished to emphasise.

In summary, there is not one gospel, in the sense of a unified story of the life of Jesus. There are the four gospels, the Gospel of Mark, the Gospel of Matthew, the Gospel of Luke and the Gospel of John, which Moloney calls 'theologically motivated narratives.'

> *Note:* Australian author, Brendan Byrne SJ, has published a series of four books, each dealing with one gospel, details of which are set out in the suggestions for further reading at the end of this work. In each of them Byrne develops this idea, that the gospels are not biographies of Jesus in the modern sense, but are theological works intended to facilitate our encounter today with the risen Lord.

The Synoptics

The Gospels of Mark, Matthew and Luke are called synoptic, (literally 'seen together'), because they share many stories, which may be placed side by side, to be compared and contrasted. Some versions of the New Testament, such as in the New Jerusalem Bible, have side notes that give references to the corresponding passages in the other Gospels. For example, beside the parable of the sower in Luke 8:4-8, references are given to the similar story in Mark 4:1-9 and Matthew 13:1-9.

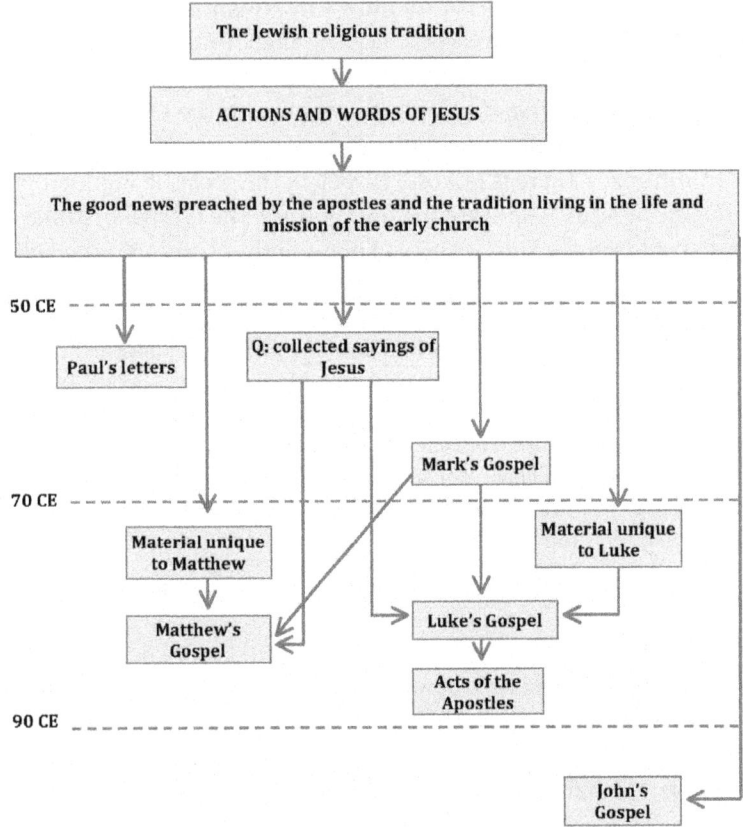

Fig. 14.2

Although the matter is still not free from controversy, most scholars now agree that the earliest Gospel was that of Mark, who relied for his material upon the oral tradition of the early church and its liturgical life. Matthew and Luke wrote independently of each other, but both obviously used Mark as one of their sources, in addition to what they each received from the oral and liturgical traditions available to them.

Scholars have also identified a large amount of material that is common to both Matthew and Luke, but which does not appear in Mark. It is sufficiently consistent for them to put forward the hypothesis that it comes from one, probably written, source, which they have identified as Q, after the German word *quelle*, meaning source.

The study of the sources on which the evangelists relied is called 'source criticism'. In the context of Biblical studies the word 'criticism' does not have the pejorative meaning of censure or faultfinding, but rather of the system of analysis or judgement. There are other forms of criticism such as:

historical criticism, which involves the study of the original languages and cultures that lie behind the Bible;

textual criticism, which examines the reliability of the actual texts as they have come down to us in the physical documents;

form criticism, which classifies the forms of the various incidents narrated in the Gospels and compares them with similar forms in the literatures of contemporary religions and cultures;

redaction criticism, which concentrates on the editing carried out by the author on the materials available to him; and

narrative criticism, which examines each Gospel as a whole story, focusing on its literary features.

These distinctions may be confusing at this stage, and my descriptions are by no means complete or necessarily accurate. These matters are discussed much more lucidly and comprehensively in Moloney's book. I suggest that for present purposes all we need to bear in mind is that the evangelists did not merely cut and paste materials from their sources. They were each relying on a living and dynamic tradition and they chose and shaped material available to them in such a way as to make a particular theological point about the Christ event.

Chapter 15
The Gospel according to Mark

Fig. 15.1

There is no mention in this gospel, or indeed in any of the others, of the name of the author, nor are there many clues to his identity. The author obviously did not think it important for his purposes that we should know who he was or much about him.

Writing at about the beginning of the fourth century, the great historian of the early Church, Eusebius, referred back to a statement by Papias of Hierapolis early in the second century, identifying as the author Peter's companion in Rome, Mark, who 'having become Peter's interpreter wrote down accurately whatever he remembered of what was said or done by the Lord, however not in order'. That tradition was unchallenged until recent times, so that the Gospel was sometimes referred to as 'the Gospel of Peter'.

It has not been demonstrated that this tradition is wrong. However, for various reasons that need not concern us at present, modern scholars generally do not rely on it. What is clear, however, as Brown points out, is 'first, that the Marcan gospel was so acceptable within a decade as to be known and approved as a guide by Matthew and Luke writing in different areas; second, that John could be independent of Mark and still have similarities to it in outline and some contents.'

This gospel does not seem to me to have been written as a book, in the way that Luke's gospel and Acts undoubtedly were. It reads more like a script for a performance that had been developed over many presentations (with some elements that might have been inserted or left out, depending on the audience) and then preserved in its relatively final form. The author was the performer, perhaps an itinerant preacher who would proclaim his good news (in old English 'god spell') after a eucharistic meal in some house church, quite possibly in Rome. Of all the Gospels, it is the one that is most obviously designed to be listened to as it is being dramatically declaimed, rather than to be read silently at leisure.

The date of its publication in relatively final form is not easy to determine. Many scholars make a good case for the late 60s. Although Jesus foretells in chapter 13 the destruction of the Temple, which did occur in 70 CE, the context could indicate that for Mark that was an event which was yet to happen.

The audience had already heard a lot about Jesus, and were probably mostly gentiles who had been converted by people who were at least familiar with aspects of Judaism. Mark assumes knowledge about the Hebrew Scriptures and religious terms, but finds it useful to remind the audience about some aspects of Jewish purity laws. They probably expected Christ's second coming sooner rather than later, and may well have experienced persecution, which fits in with the suggested date.

As a drama, Mark's Gospel divides into four parts. There is a short prologue, followed by three acts. The first act depicts Jesus' mission in and around Galilee. The second portrays a journey to Jerusalem, while the final act is set in Jerusalem.

The prologue (1:1–13)

Mark announces his purpose succinctly. This is only a beginning, not just of his presentation, but of the Good News, which can mean the good news about Jesus, or the good news that Jesus brings. In either case, the message is that Jesus is the Christ, the son of God.

The title of Christ comes from the Greek translation of the Hebrew word messiah. It means one who has been anointed. It has its origin in the Hebrew Scriptures, where it did not have a defined technical meaning, being used of David, and of other kings, priests and prophets. In the first century, it could not be said that the whole Jewish people expected the coming of a single figure called the Messiah, but many did hope for what Fitzmyer called 'an anointed agent sent by God either in the Davidic, kingly or political tradition for the restoration of Israel and the triumph of God's power and dominion, or in the priestly tradition.' Naturally, many would have hoped for one who would free them from the tyranny of the pagan Romans. On the other hand, there was certainly no expectation that he would suffer and be put to death, let alone be raised from the dead.

The title, 'son of God' was not meant by Mark, nor understood by his listeners, to mean that Jesus was divine. That doctrine was to be developed and made specific much later, especially by John in his gospel. There had been references in the Hebrew Scriptures to a King, such as David, as being a 'son of God', and to a personified Israel as being son and God as being father of the nation. The title denoted a special status and relationship to God, and especially indicated someone who fully performed God's will. The title is used on a number of occasions by the unclean spirits, who are told to keep quiet about it, but the special relationship is affirmed on a number of key occasions in Mark's gospel; at Jesus' baptism (1:11), at his transfiguration (9:7), and at his death, ironically by his executioner (15:39).

Because of its association with kingship, in Mark's usage the title emphasises the role of Jesus in bringing about the Kingdom of God or Realm of God, a major theme in his gospel. The first words of Jesus that Mark reports are that 'The time is fulfilled, and the kingdom of God has come near; repent, and believe in the good news' (1:15).

The prologue also tells the audience that Jesus is Lord, he is greater than John the Baptist, he will baptise with the Holy Spirit, and he was driven by the Holy Spirit into the desert to be tested by Satan and nourished by angels.

Will the events in the drama about to be unfolded conform easily to this picture of Jesus?

Act 1 The mission in and around Galilee (1:14—8:30)

The first act rushes headlong through a series of scenes, in which Jesus establishes a number of relationships, and proceeds to a climax in which Mark sets out his view of who and what Jesus is.

He begins to gather his closest disciples, who witness many marvelous cures. He appoints the twelve, whom he sends out to proclaim repentance and to cure the sick. Despite all, they do not understand, so that sometimes he has to explain his parables to them, and at other times to upbraid them for their blindness.

> The Greek word *apostello, to send out,* gives us our word 'apostle'.

He encounters opposition from the religious leaders of Israel. The people of Nazareth reject him. His own family seeks to restrain him because people think he is mad. In response he establishes a new principle for belonging to his family, doing the will of God (3:34-35).

On a number of occasions he moves outside Jewish Galilee, into neighbouring gentile country, such as the Decapolis side of the lake, where he heals the demoniac (5:1-20), or Tyre, where he responds to the faith of the Syrophoenician woman and cures her daughter (7:24-30). His ministry is to both Jew and gentile.

Throughout this act, the question is constantly asked, 'Who is this?' The evil spirits obey him. He forgives sins. The wind and the seas obey him. The Nazarenes cannot accept that a mere village carpenter could do all these things. Herod and his Court are puzzled, and think John the Baptist has risen. The deaf hear and the mute speak. Then, significantly, at Bethsaida Jesus heals a blind man, not instantly, but in stages (8:22–26). He then puts the question directly to his disciples, 'But who do you say that I am?' Peter responds, 'You are the Messiah' (8:29). But, like the blind man, Peter does not at first see clearly.

Act 2 Journey to Jerusalem (8:31—10:52)

The second act opens with Jesus telling his disciples openly that they have the wrong idea about his being Messiah. He is to suffer and die and rise again. Peter still clings to his conventional view, and is rebuked. In this scene also Jesus develops his teaching about what is required to be a true disciple, to deny oneself, take up the cross and follow him.

The transfiguration follows. God insists that the disciples listen to Jesus, his son. The disciples discover that they have no power unless he gives it, through prayer. Again he predicts his passion, and teaches the disciples that following the sort of Messiah that he is does not provide a path to earthly power, but to a life of service and self denial, especially in the difficult areas of marriage and possessions.

Jesus predicts his passion a third time, and James and John demonstrate that they still do not understand. They seek positions of honour. Again Jesus teaches that to be a disciple they must follow him to service and the cross. A second blind man shows that unconditional faith leads immediately to sight.

Act 3 Jerusalem, death and the empty tomb (11:1—16:8)

In the first scene, Mark describes Jesus entering Jerusalem in terms that recall Old Testament prophecy and Psalm 118, and again people misunderstand. He has not come to restore the kingdom of David, but of God.

Next, he enters the temple, and proclaims the end of the Temple cult, as symbolised by the cursing and the withering of the fig tree.

In its place he teaches the way of faith, prayer and forgiveness. He demolishes the authority of the religious leaders by his answers to their trap questions. One of the Scribes agrees to his teaching, and after that no one dared question him (12:28-34).

He foretells the destruction of Jerusalem and the persecution of its people (13:1-23). But that will not be the end of the world, because first the gospel must be proclaimed to all the nations (13:7-10). Then he speaks of the signs leading to the end of human history (13:24-37).

The climax approaches rapidly. The authorities decide to kill Jesus. He is anointed. Judas agrees to betray him. He shares his last meal with his disciples, and foretells his abandonment by them, especially by Peter. In his distress at Gethsemane he bows to the will of his father while the disciples sleep. He is arrested and they all flee.

Jesus is tried, first before the council, where the false witnesses are unable to construct coherent evidence, but Jesus solves his enemies' problem by agreeing that he is the Messiah. Meanwhile Peter denies him three times. Next he is taken before Pilate, who, wishing to satisfy the angry mob, hands him over to be crucified. It is as 'King of the Jews' that he is tortured and executed (15:2, 9, 12, 18, 26, 32).

The same women who saw the body of Jesus placed in the tomb go there with spices to anoint him. They find that the stone sealing the tomb had already been rolled back. A young man in a white robe tells them that Jesus has been raised, and orders them to tell Peter and the disciples to go to meet him in Galilee. Instead they flee in terror and tell no one.

This last scene is remarkable. Most scholars now agree that Mark's original Gospel ended at 16:8, and that later editors added the shorter and longer additional endings that we find in our Bibles.

Those who first heard this ending would have been aware of the tradition later to be recorded by the other evangelists, namely that the women received the Easter message and delivered it to the disciples. They would be struck by Mark's deliberate changing of that tradition. Why did he do that? He wants to make the point that what Jesus said would happen, did happen. That has been true of all the predictions that he has made in Mark's Gospel. At the last supper he had said, 'after I am raised up, I will go before you to Galilee' (14:26). The young man in the tomb repeats the prediction (16:7).

Mark's audience knows that he did so, or they would not be listening to this gospel. There is no need to place Jesus' meeting with Peter and the disciples in Galilee within the confines of the story. Mark is linking the end of his gospel with the prologue, which told of God's sending of his son to proclaim the good news of the coming of his kingdom.

- *What three important things about Jesus does Mark tell us in his gospel?*

Chapter 16
2 Thessalonians

The Deutero-Pauline letters

We saw in chapter 5 that there is a group of seven letters that almost all scholars agree were written by Paul himself. Then there is a group of three, called Deutero-Pauline. That does not mean that there is any certainty that these were not written by Paul. In each case there are continuing disputes, with eminent scholars on each side of the debate. It is difficult to see that there will ever be finality to the debate. Does it matter?

In ancient times 'author' may sometimes have meant the authority behind a work, rather than our modern idea of one who is responsible not only for the ideas but also for the words in which they are expressed. There is justification for this in the Hebrew Scriptures, where, for example, books about the Law were attributed to Moses, because he was the great lawgiver, and psalms were attributed to David since he was renowned as a composer of songs to the Lord.

If they were not actually composed or dictated by Paul, these letters were written by followers of Paul, who wrote in his name because they were confident that what they wrote was what Paul would have said in their situation had he still been alive. Naturally, in such a case, they would imitate Paul's style or use such language that their readers would react, 'Yes, that's just the way he would have said it'. Such a letter is called 'pseudonymous', or written under an assumed name.

In any event, the original readers would have known the truth about their provenance, and no one was being misled. We should accept these letters as part of Scripture with some connection to Paul. As Brown remarks, 'Moreover, keeping open both possibilities challenges readers to think more perceptively about the issues involved'.

Who wrote 2 Thessalonians?

On the question of the authenticity of 2 Thessalonians Brown writes, 'Scholars are almost evenly divided on whether Paul wrote it, although the view that he did not seems to be gaining ground even among moderates'. After discussing the arguments for and against, he writes, 'personally I cannot decide with certitude'.

The letter purports to be from Paul, Silvanus and Timothy. If Paul wrote the letter, he probably sent it to the Church in Thessalonica shortly after 1 Thessalonians, in about 51 or 52 CE. If it was pseudonymous, it would be dated to later in the 1st Century, and may have been intended for a wider audience.

The structure

The opening is in the classic Pauline style, wishing for the readers grace and peace from God our Father and the Lord Jesus Christ, and giving thanks for their faith and love. Their faithfulness under persecution will save them, and their persecutors will be punished, when Christ comes again.

In 1 Thessalonians, Paul had addressed concerns about this second coming of Jesus Christ. This letter deals with the same concerns; perhaps to reassure its readers that the end was not as imminent as some seemed to fear. A number of apocalyptic signs, mysterious to us, must happen before that day comes. The letter confronts the danger that false prophecy poses to the community.

After thanksgiving, prayer and a request for prayer, the body of the letter concludes with a warning against idleness, which might have resulted from a mistaken belief that there was only a short time left and that work was useless. The letter concludes with a purported signature and the customary blessing.

Chapter 17
Colossians

The Colossians lived in a city on an important commercial route through the Phrygian mountains, about 180 km (120 miles) east of Ephesus in southwest Turkey. Nearby were two other notable cities, Laodicea and Hierapolis.

Fig. 17.1
Map of Asia Minor (present-day Turkey) showing the town of Colossae. Smyrna is present-day Izmir

They had not been evangelised by Paul, but the letter assumes that the Christians in each of the three towns formed a close-knit community.

It may have been formed by Epaphras, a native of Colossae and a close associate of Paul (1:7; 4:12). Onesimus, and perhaps also his master, Philemon, were Colossians (4:9). It seems that Paul's letter to Philemon had the desired effect, and he had sent Onesimus back to Paul, who had then sent him out on mission.

Did Paul write this letter?

The tradition that he did was unbroken from the 2nd to the 19th century. Since then controversy has raged over the issue, focusing on two areas of comparison with the undoubted Pauline letters, namely language and style, and theological ideas. Brown writes that at present 60 percent of critical scholarship holds that he did not, but that no assurance is possible. Having read his outline of the arguments, I incline to the view that, if it cannot be said that Paul did write this letter, it is certainly possible. I am, for example, impressed by the number of fellow workers whom he details in 4:7–17, which goes well beyond what another author might think necessary to give corroborative detail to a fiction.

If Paul did not write it, the letter was probably written about 70 to 80 CE, by someone who knew the Pauline tradition extremely well, and probably from Ephesus. If Paul did write it, he was in prison at the time (4:10), and the developed theology and similarities to Romans favour a date about 61–63 CE, and from Rome. In either case, as Brown comments, 'In its vision of Christ, of his body the church, and of the mystery of God hidden for ages, Colossians is truly majestic, and certainly a worthy representative of the Pauline heritage'.

Structure

The letter begins with the customary salutation (1:1–2) and prayer of thanksgiving (1:3–12). Epaphras has painted an encouraging picture of the way in which the Colossians have received the gospel.

The body of the letter begins with a poetic passage on the supremacy of Christ, thought by many to have been based on a contemporaneous hymn (1:13–20), followed by an exhortation to his readers (1:21–23). Paul's own mission is then described (1:24–2:7), no doubt to reinforce the authority of the warning about false teachings that follows (2:8–23). Those teachings seem to have related to a mixture of pagan and Jewish ideas.

A section of spiritual advice based on their new life in Christ (3:1–17) is followed by some practical advice for Christian households (3:18–4:6), which must be understood in the light of the culture of the first century. Even so, a new motivation is introduced into the relationships between husbands and wives, parents and children, and masters and slaves, namely 'in the Lord' (3:18, 20), 'Lord' (3:22, 24), and 'Master in Heaven' (4:1).

The letter concludes with detailed final greetings and messages (4:7–17), and Paul's signature and blessing (4:18).

Chapter 18
Ephesians

By contrast with Colossians, Paul's authorship of this letter was queried as early as in the 16th century, by Erasmus, who remarked on the differences between its style and that of the undoubted Pauline letters. Arguments against Paul's authorship became systematic during the 19th century.

For example, although Paul had spent 3 years in Ephesus (Acts 20:31), there is no greeting or reference by name to any of the many friends and fellow workers whom he must have known there, and in 3:2 the author merely assumes that the readers had heard of Paul's ministry.

The phrase, 'in Ephesus', in 1:1 is missing from a number of early and important manuscripts, and may have been added by later copyists to a letter which was really addressed to a wider audience. It is possible that the letter was an early form of encyclical, destined for several churches in western Asia Minor (modern Turkey). The letter would then have been addressed 'To the saints who are also faithful in Christ Jesus'.

Brown's assessment is that at present about 80 percent of scholars hold that it was written by a follower of Paul. He suggests as a plausible theory that 'someone in the Ephesian School of Paul's disciples produced it as an encouraging portrayal of aspects of Pauline thought'. Imaginative suggestions, which can be no more than guesses, include Onesimus, Timothy, Tichycus and even Luke. On this hypothesis the letter could be dated to about the 90s.

What is certain is that the author was steeped in Paul's theology, being described as his 'supreme interpreter' and 'best disciple'. The letter has been called 'the crown of Paulinism', and only Romans has exercised as much influence on Christian thought and spirituality.

The earlier, undisputed, Pauline letters were written to particular churches, confronting their specific problems. Paul was expecting an early second coming of Christ, and had to contend with differences between pagan converts and Jewish Christians, who insisted on circumcision and adherence to the Law of Moses. Such issues do not trouble the writer of Ephesians. There is no evidence in the letter of any wrong ideas or contentious matters affecting the recipients.

The body of the faithful is seen as 'the church', in which Jews and gentiles have been made one in Christ, a body of which Christ is the head (1:20–23; 2:13–22). The Pauline tradition is preserved. Salvation is still achieved, not by works, but by faith, which is the gift of God, but 'we are what he has made us, created in Christ Jesus for good works, which God prepared beforehand to be our way of life' (2:8-10). There is no need to emphasise the second coming, because Christ has already achieved so much through his church (3:5-6).

The opening greeting (1:1–2)

This was followed by the usual prayer of thanksgiving (1:3-23). The writer, speaking as Paul, rejoices with his readers in God's plan to unite all creation in Christ. He gives thanks that they had heard the Good News, believed, and received the Holy Spirit.

The body of the letter

The first part is largely an exposition of doctrine (2:1—3:21). The writer and his readers had once been dead through sin, but God had brought them to life in Christ by his gift of grace (2:1-10).

This joyful message is then applied particularly to the gentiles. Christ has broken down the dividing wall between Jew and gentile so that now all are one in one body, in Christ (2:11-22). Paul had received a special commission from God for them, so that the mystery of Christ, in which all are united in him, might be manifested through the church (3:1-13). The section concludes with a magnificent prayer and praise of God (3:14-20).

Next in the body of the letter is an exposition of the implication that God's plan has for our behaviour, so that we might lead a life worthy of our calling (4:1—6:20). There is a list of seven manifestations of oneness in the Christian life (4:4-6), then a list of diverse gifts given by the risen Christ for building up the one, whole, body of Christ in love (4:7-16).

Having grown up into being part of the body of which Christ is the head, and being members of one another, readers are exhorted to put away their old way of life, and to live as imitators of God (4:17—5:20).

The household relationships, those between wives and husbands, children and parents, slaves and masters, are redefined in the light of their relationships with Christ (5:21-6:9). This whole code is governed by the guiding principle in 5:21—they are each to be subject to one another out of reverence for Christ. The passage is the more radical because pressure is directed to the one who has authority and power. In the culture of the time there may have been nothing new in telling wives to be subject to their husbands. But the relationship is now to be seen as like that between Christ and his church, which is subject to Christ, not because of power, but because of love. And it is the husband who is to be like Christ, who 'loved the church and gave himself up for her' (5:25).

The final exhortation

This is expressed in the metaphors of battle, where, in the struggle against the forces of evil, it is the armour of God that will enable victory (6:10-17). The writer asks for prayers for himself, and ends with a brief reference to Tychicus (as in Col 4:7), and a benediction (6:18-23).

Chapter 19
The Gospel according to Matthew

Fig. 19.1

For most of us, the Gospel of Matthew is probably the one with which we are most familiar. It is placed first amongst the gospels in our Bibles. Until the liturgical changes that followed Vatican II it was the one most often used in the gospel readings on Sundays. It is the source of our most widely used version of the Lord's Prayer, and the Sermon on the Mount provides the most extended version of the Lord's teaching about Christian behaviour. It has been called 'the church's gospel' because it is the source of the teaching authority of the church and of Peter's central place in it. It was the gospel that was most readily accepted during the development of the canon of the New Testament.

Yet, despite the fact that we are familiar with the details of many episodes in the gospel, it will be a new experience for most of us to read it as a whole. The writer had a plan—he designed the gospel with a plot, in order to communicate a particular theological point of view to his readers, a point of view that is relevant to us today.

Who wrote it and when?

The title 'according to Matthew' was being attached to copies of this gospel by the latter half of the second century. The great early church historian Eusebius (263–339 CE) records an early second century tradition that Matthew 'arranged in order the sayings in the Hebrew language', which led to a long-standing view that the apostle Matthew originally wrote the gospel in Aramaic, and it was then translated into Greek. Margaret Monro followed this tradition in her book.

Nevertheless Brown concludes that it is best to accept the position, now common amongst modern scholars, that the gospel was originally written in Greek, by an author who was not an eyewitness, and who depended for his sources largely on Mark and the inferred source Q, together with the oral tradition available to him.

More contentious, but also in Brown's view more probable, is the view that he was a Jewish Christian. The gospel has been called 'the most Jewish of the Gospels'. The author's frequent use of the Hebrew Scriptures shows that he knew Hebrew and probably Aramaic, and there are numerous features of Jewish thought and theology throughout the gospel, such as the genealogy, the comparison of Jesus with Moses, and the modifications of the Law in the Sermon on the Mount.

The author's use of the Greek language is more sophisticated than Mark's. He tones down passages derived from Mark that might appear disrespectful. He obviously did not think it necessary that we should know a great deal about himself. Perhaps the closest that he comes to a reference to himself is the statement by Jesus at 13:52, 'Therefore every scribe who has been trained for the kingdom of heaven is like the master of a household who brings out of his treasure what is new and what is old'.

The date of composition is also still contentious. Most agree that it was after 70 CE and before 100 CE . Brown's conclusion is that 80–90 CE is the most plausible dating, but that the arguments are not precise.

For whom was he writing?

Early tradition placed Matthew in Palestine, but the majority of experts now think that the community was located in Syria, and specifically in Antioch. When the Christians were scattered after the martyrdom of Stephen, Antioch became one of the main Christian centres, associated with the mission to the gentiles of Paul and Barnabas, and the site of the disagreement over Jewish food laws. It is likely that a church that was initially strongly and conservatively Jewish had become mixed and, over decades, increasingly gentile in composition. However, the author and his readers obviously understood the Jewish world and its traditions. Matthew quoted Jewish Scriptures frequently, and used Hebrew as well as Greek sources for his quotations.

But their world was radically different from that of the Apostles and the early converts from Jerusalem. Over the centuries before the time of Christ Judaism had developed into a religion centred upon worship in the temple in Jerusalem. As Acts makes clear, the earliest Christians continued to frequent the Temple, and they could regard themselves, as Paul did, simply as Jews who believed that Jesus was the Messiah.

During the 60s, Peter and Paul had been executed in Rome, and James in Jerusalem. A Jewish revolt against the Romans began in

66 CE. In 70 CE, Rome had brutally crushed the revolt, destroying the Temple, and carrying off the sacred objects to be paraded in the conqueror's triumph in Rome. Without the Temple, the Jewish people were forced to find a different way of worship. Within a fairly short time, under the leadership of the Rabbis, the sages of Israel, they concentrated on observance of the Law and communal prayer in the synagogues.

It was not long before the leaders of this new form of Judaism decided that it was not compatible with Christianity, and excluded Christians from their synagogues. Many passages in the gospel suggest separation of the community from Judaism. A major reason for this gospel may well have been that it was written as a response to this development.

Mark's gospel had finished with an empty tomb and terrified disciples. Matthew's concludes with a risen Lord proclaiming his authority, sending his followers out to make disciples of all the nations and promising to be with them to the end of time. His is a different community from Paul's Thessalonians, who were so concerned about the imminent return of the Lord and the end of time, or his Galatians, worrying about whether they had to become Jews in order to be Christians.

Resolving a seeming contradiction

However, one of their central concerns was their relationship with Judaism. In dealing with this concern, Matthew seems at first sight to be inconsistent. At 5:17-18 Jesus says that he had not come to abolish the law and the prophets, and that not a jot of the law would pass away until heaven and earth should pass away. He sent his twelve Apostles only to the 'lost sheep of Israel' (10:5-6). He told the gentile woman who wanted him to heal her daughter, 'I was sent only to the lost sheep of Israel' (15:24). Although he denounced the behaviour of the Scribes and Pharisees he told his disciples, 'The Scribes and Pharisees sit on Moses' seat: therefore do whatever they teach you and follow it; but do not do as they do, for they do not practice what they preach' (23:2-3).

Yet there is tension even within the gospel. At 8:5-13 Matthew tells of the healing of the centurion's servant. His faith is held up as an example to Israel, and while many of the heirs to the kingdom will be cast out, many will come from the East and the West to eat with Abraham. Despite what he says to her about the exclusiveness of his mission, Jesus heals the gentile woman's daughter because of her faith (15:28). At the end of the gospel Jesus claims that all authority in heaven and on earth is his. He replaces the rite of initiation of circumcision with baptism in the name of the Father and of the Son and of the Holy Spirit. His disciples are to go, not just to Israel, but to all nations, and to teach them to obey, not the Torah, but his commands. This commission contradicts much that is central to Jewish belief and doctrine.

There may well have been within the community some who held that the church must live under the Law, while others argued that the teachings of Jesus sufficed for Jewish and gentile converts.

How does Matthew resolve this seeming conflict?

The answer lies in the way Matthew uses time in his story. The Lord's instructions to his followers early in the gospel to obey the Jewish law and those at the end of the gospel to go beyond it were each valid for the time at which they were given. Something was to happen in the gospel story to change radically the role of Jesus and his disciples. That event was to be his death and resurrection.

When Jesus said, 'Do not think I have come to abolish the Law or the prophets', he added, 'I have come not to abolish but to fulfil'. He then said, not only, 'until heaven and earth pass away, not one letter, not one iota, will pass from the law', but he also added, 'until all is accomplished' (5:17-18).

What did Matthew mean by heaven and earth passing away? What did he mean by all being accomplished? It could not mean the end of all history, as that would render meaningless the Lord's commission to the disciples at the end of the gospel. Matthew has adopted some traditional apocalyptic symbols from Hebrew Scripture, and changed their timing. They occur in two passages.

Describing the death of Jesus, Matthew wrote, 'From noon on, darkness came over the whole land until three in the afternoon. Then Jesus cried again with a loud voice and breathed his last. At that moment the curtain of the Temple was torn in two, from top to bottom. The earth shook, and the rocks were split. The tombs also were opened and many bodies of the saints who had fallen asleep were raised' (27:45, 50-52).

In the second passage, describing the events surrounding the resurrection, he wrote, 'And suddenly there was a great earthquake; for an angel of the Lord, descending from heaven, came and rolled back the stone and sat on it. His appearance was like lightning, and his clothing white as snow' (28:2-3).

According to Matthew, not only will these apocalyptic signs, such as the darkening of the skies, the tearing of the Temple curtain, the earth shaking, rocks splitting, the dead rising, the appearance of an angel, take place at the end of history, they have already happened as Jesus died and was raised. Not only has heaven and earth passed away, but all is accomplished. That was the turning point of the ages. In his lifetime Jesus had lived in accordance with the Law. In his life, death and resurrection he had fulfilled it perfectly. Historical Israel had lost its way, and the church that Jesus founded is the new Israel.

Structure of the story

Many commentators have focused on the five great discourses in the gospel as indicating its structure. They are:
the sermon on the Mount (5:1—7:28);
the missionary discourse (10:5—11:1);
the parable discourse (13:1-53);
the church discourse (18:1-35) and
the discourse on the end of time (24:1—25:46).

Moloney points out that such an analysis does not give sufficient attention to the surrounding narrative. He suggests that the plot unfolds in six major narrative units.

1 The coming of the Messiah (1:1—4:16)

The genealogy, the annunciation to Joseph, the visit of the wise men, the flight into Egypt and the return to Nazareth together show that the birth of Jesus is the fulfilment of God's promise made through the prophets. John the Baptist proclaims the fact and the voice from heaven confirms it. Satan tests Jesus in the wilderness to see if he is the son of God and is defeated. Jesus leaves Nazareth and makes his home in Capernaum in further fulfilment of prophecy.

2 The messianic ministry of Jesus to Israel (4:17—11:1)

In three places Matthew makes explicit the essential theme of this section. It is the messianic ministry of Jesus to Israel, preaching, teaching and healing (4:23, 9:35, 11:1).

After recruiting his first four key disciples, Simon Peter, Andrew, James and John, he preached the Sermon on the Mount. Not only is the mountain significant; what Matthew reports Jesus as saying is also crucial. After teaching the Beatitudes, and denying any intention of abolishing the Law of Moses, on six occasions Jesus contrasts the old law ('it was said in ancient times') with his own commandments ('but I say to you'). He does not loosen the bonds of the Law, instead he sets the standard of behaviour even higher, with respect to anger (5:21–26), adultery (5:27–30), divorce (5:31–32), oaths (5:33–37), retaliation (5:38–42) and love for enemies (5:43–48). This is a clear depiction by Matthew of Jesus as the successor to Moses as lawgiver. The other well-known teachings in chapters 6 and 7 are given in this context.

A series of nine miracles in chapters 8 and 9 demonstrates his power in deed as well as in word. This power fulfils a prophecy made by Isaiah (8:16–17).

In chapter 10 Jesus commissions his apostles and sends them on mission exclusively to 'the lost sheep of the house of Israel' (10:5–6). Then follows the discourse on mission (10:5–11:1).

However, scattered in this section are hints of what is to come. Jesus contrasts the teachings of the Pharisees with their behaviour (5:20; 6:5, 16). The crowds appreciate the authority of his teaching, by contrast with that of the Scribes (7:28–29; 9:33). He holds up the faith of the Centurion as an example to Israel (8:10–13). The Pharisees complain that Jesus casts out demons by the power of the devil (9:34). Jesus warns the disciples that their mission will be opposed and will cause division and hatred (10:16–25, 34–36).

3 Crisis and development in the Messiah's ministry (11:2—16:12)

At the beginning of this section it is John the Baptist who poses the question that is central to it, namely, is Jesus really the Messiah? (11:3). Jesus gives John his answer (11:4-6), but will Israel accept it?

Jesus complains that his generation does not appreciate him (11:16-19), and even the cities where he worked most of his miracles have not repented (11:20-24). On the other hand the truth has been revealed to his disciples, to infants rather than to the wise, and Jesus contrasts the lightness of his burden with that on those who do not accept him (11:25-30).

The Pharisees challenge him about plucking grain and curing a man with a withered hand on the Sabbath, and when he defies them they begin plotting to kill him (12:1-14). Matthew now introduces directly the idea that the mission of Jesus to the gentiles will be in fulfilment of a prophecy (12:15-21). Jesus meets the challenge by the Pharisees to the legitimacy of his healing power with a withering demolition of their argument (12:22-37). They ask for a sign from him, to be given only a forecast of his death and resurrection, followed again by a condemnation of their refusal to repent (12:38-45).

The rift between Jesus and the leaders of Israel becomes explicit in chapter 13. He speaks now only in parables, because they will not listen or understand, whereas his disciples do (13:9-17). Again a prophecy is being fulfilled (13:14-15, 35). He is rejected even in his hometown (13:54-58). Three times Matthew summarises what is happening. Jesus is withdrawing, first from where the Pharisees are plotting to kill him (12:14-16), then from Nazareth after hearing about the murder of John the Baptist (14:13), and, most significantly, after demolishing the Pharisees and Scribes and their petty traditions (15:1-20), to the gentile territory of Tyre and Sidon where he cures the daughter of the Canaanite woman because of her faith (14:21-28).

The strength of her faith may be contrasted with the frailty of that of his disciples, especially Peter (14:26-33). After Jesus has worked two bread miracles the Pharisees and Sadducees still ask him for a sign, and when Jesus tells his disciples to beware of the yeast of the Pharisees and Sadducees, their faith is so weak that they do not understand, and he has to explain to them that he is warning them against their teachings (16:1-12).

4 The Messiah's journey to Jerusalem (16:13—20:34)

The event that links this narrative unit with the previous one, and also controls what is to follow, was also a central feature in Mark's gospel. It is the confession of Peter that Jesus is the Messiah. Matthew adds to Mark's account that he is also the Son of the Living God. In addition, Jesus responds by speaking, for the first time, about founding a church, to be built upon Peter, and against which the gates of hell will not prevail (16:13-19). This proclamation by Peter is the definitive answer to the question posed by John the Baptist at the beginning of the previous section.

However, Jesus must now begin the long and difficult task of persuading the disciples that he is not the type of Messiah that they have grown up to expect. He is to suffer at the hands of the leaders of Israel, to be killed, and to be raised (16:21). Their discipleship also will lead to rejection, suffering and even death (16:24-26). The disciples will demonstrate on a number of occasions that they have not understood his message. Peter is the first to be rebuked (16:22-23).

Jesus is to repeat his prediction of suffering and death on two more occasions (17:22-23; 20:17-19). Peter, James and John witness the Transfiguration (17:1-8), yet demonstrate the frailty of their faith by their inability to cure the boy with a demon (17:14-21).

In chapter 18 Matthew collates the teachings of Jesus about the life and order of the church, and the necessity for humility and forgiveness in its members.

Leaving Galilee, Jesus leads his disciples south to Judea, towards Jericho, on the way to Jerusalem. He instructs them on his difficult doctrines about marriage and wealth, achievable only with God's help (19:1-26). His promise of eternal reward to those who follow him is tempered by his statement that 'many who are first will be last and the last will be first', exemplified in his parable about the labourers in the vineyard (19:27—20:16).

A third time he predicts his passion, but the disciples still do not understand. The mother of James and John still seeks advancement for them, angering the others, so Jesus has to tell them again that to follow him must involve service and self-sacrifice (20:17-28). Their lack of faith is contrasted with the faith of the two blind men on the roadside at Jericho, who, despite opposition, call out in faith to Jesus as son of David. He cures their blindness and they follow him (20:29-34).

Thus this narrative unit, which began with Peter's declaration that Jesus was the Messiah, concludes with the acceptance of it by the two blind men.

5 Death and resurrection of the Messiah (21:1—28:15).

This unit begins in triumph, and proceeds through confrontation, conflict, betrayal and disaster to ultimate vindication and victory.

Matthew depicts the entry of Jesus into Jerusalem as an obvious fulfillment of prophecies about the coming of the Messiah (21:1-11).

What happens next sets the scene for everything that is to follow. Jesus cleanses the Temple and cures the blind and the lame in it, a demonstration of messianic power reinforced by the instant withering of the barren fig tree (21:12-22). When the chief priests and elders challenge his authority he confronts them with a justified refusal to answer, followed by two parables that pointedly accuse them and the Pharisees, and predicts the removal from them of the kingdom of God. For the time being fear of the crowds is all that prevents them from arresting him (21:23-46).

Honour was even more important in society at that time than it is for us now. The authorities had lost face in their last encounter with Jesus. Not daring to arrest him, they set out to humiliate him.

The Pharisees lose the first encounter when Jesus turns their trick question about taxes back on them (22:15-22). Then the Sadducees are ridiculed about their infantile ideas of the Resurrection (22:23-33). Jesus passes the test question set for him by a lawyer about the greatest commandment of all, but they are unable to answer his question about the Messiah's being both David's son and his Lord. They retire from the field, comprehensively defeated (22:34-46).

In a dramatic series of seven 'Woes', Jesus proceeds to denounce the Scribes and Pharisees, especially for their concentration on external observances, while neglecting justice and mercy (23:1-36). He cries out in anguish at the failure of Jerusalem, (that is, Judaism in general), to listen to his saving message, and foretells the destruction of the Temple (23:37-24:2).

Then he warns his disciples against being led astray, and, in another apocalyptic passage, he tries to strengthen them to withstand the many things that must happen before the end of time and his second coming (24:3–35). As with many apocalyptic passages, it is difficult to discern an exact timeline or sequence of things that are to happen, but there is obviously to be a time in between, during which they must be watchful, illustrated by the parables of the ten bridesmaids and of the talents (24:36–25:30), and his description of the last judgement, when the criterion of our success or failure will be our love of our fellow man, especially of the poor and needy (25:31–46).

The time for teaching is now over. Passover will be in two days time, and the leaders of the people, unable to withstand their confrontation and denunciation by Jesus, have decided on murder, when the time is right (26:1–5).

Jesus is anointed for burial (26:6–13). Judas betrays him (26:14–16). He eats the Passover meal with his disciples and institutes the Eucharist (26:17–29). The agony in the Garden and his arrest follow. His disciples desert him and flee (26:30–56).

At his trial before the high priest he is proclaimed and condemned as Messiah and Son of God (26:57–67). At his trial before Pilate he is identified both as King of the Jews (27:11, 29) and as Messiah (27:17, 22).

The people, under the influence of their leaders, reject him and choose a false pretender, Barabbas (27:15–23) and Pilate delivers him up to be crucified. During his passion he is mocked as Son of God (27:40, 43) and as King of the Jews (27:29, 42) and the official charge against him displayed on the cross identifies him as King of the Jews (27:36). Yet it is the pagan Centurion and his soldiers who, observing the earthquake and other phenomena that accompany his death proclaim, 'Truly this man was God's Son' (27:51–54).

Jesus is buried and the elders take steps to have the tomb guarded (27:55–66). As Jesus had foretold, God raises him on the third day. The women discover the empty tomb, and receive the good news of the Resurrection from the angel. While they are hastening to tell the disciples, they meet the risen Lord, who instructs them to tell the disciples to meet him in Galilee (28:1–10).

The unit ends with a refutation of the excuses that were obviously being spread by Jewish authorities in Matthew's time to explain away the claims made by Christians about the resurrection. The opposition of the old Israel to the Messiah is complete and final (28:11–15).

6 The Messiah's commission to his disciples (28:16-20)

The disciples gather in Galilee as instructed and meet Jesus, again on a mountain, where typically commandments are handed down. The future begins as it will continue, with Jesus being worshipped, but some doubting (28:16–17).

The gospel is to be preached not only to Israel. Jesus commissions them to make disciples of all nations. For the first time in the New Testament we have an explicit statement about the Trinity, Father, Son and Holy Spirit, in whose name the new rite of initiation is to be performed. The commandments that are to be obeyed are his commandments. He promises to be with them always, to the end of time (28:18–20).

In summary

- Matthew was writing for a community that had recently been forcibly separated from the exclusive and unique milieu of Judaism in which most of them had grown up. Many perhaps longed for the old ways and the companionship of the synagogue, and were unsure about what their relationship should be with the surrounding gentile world.

- Matthew set out to show the central part that Jesus had played in God's plan for the salvation of humankind. God first revealed himself to Abraham, from whom the people of Israel were descended. He had given them his Law through the prophet Moses. Through many of his prophets God had promised to Israel a Messiah, to be a descendant of King David. Jesus was that Messiah, a second Moses and lawgiver. But not only was he descended from David, he was God's own son. In his life he had lived perfectly the true Law of God. Israel had rejected Jesus, refusing to accept him as Messiah.

- The death and resurrection of Jesus marked a turning point in the history of Israel and of God's plan. The true Israel from then on was to consist of the followers of Jesus, called by him his church. He commissioned that church to go out to preach his gospel of salvation to all mankind. The characteristics of a true follower of Jesus are love of neighbour and preparedness for service and self-sacrifice.

- *What three important things about Jesus does Matthew tell us in his Gospel?*

Chapter 20
Hebrews

Who wrote the Letter to the Hebrews?

In my Douai version of the Bible, this work is headed, 'The Epistle of St Paul to the Hebrews'. You will find the same heading in the King James Version, and Margaret Monro follows the same tradition in her book, *Enjoying the New Testament*.

The tradition is ancient. Acceptance into the canon of authoritative works in the early church often depended on a connection with the apostles, and Hebrews was being attributed to Paul by some by the end of the 2nd century. Timothy is mentioned in it (13:23), and there are connections between Hebrews and Romans and other Pauline letters.

Doubts were expressed early by ancient scholars. Origen (184-253) remarked that only God knows who wrote Hebrews. Tertullian (166-220) attributed it to Barnabas. Even in translation the style of writing is different from that in the undoubted Pauline letters. In the original Greek the differences are even more marked. Paul always insisted that he received his gospel directly from the Lord, not from other human beings (Gal 1:11-12). Yet the author of Hebrews states that the message was declared first by the Lord and 'attested to us by those who heard him' (2:3). Scholarly opinion now agrees almost entirely with Origen, that the work is anonymous.

However, we can know some things about the author from the evidence of the work itself.

He had a Greek background. The Greek that he wrote has a sonority and elegance that is not matched in any other New Testament writing. He obviously had a good education and demonstrates a mastery of Hellenistic rhetoric, together with some knowledge of Greek philosophy.

He had a Jewish background. He had an intimate and extensive knowledge of the Jewish Scriptures in the Greek translation known as the Septuagint. His argument is based on ideas derived from Jewish history, ritual and priesthood.

He was a Christian, who wrote with authority. Timothy was a companion in his ministry. He knew the people to whom he was writing and had been separated from them for a time, but hoped to rejoin them soon, possibly together with Timothy (13:19, 23).

To whom was he writing?

The letter was obviously not written to the Jewish people generally, nor is it an attempt to convert people who were Jews. The title was not supplied by the author, but by a later editor, probably because the content dealt in such detail with Jewish liturgy and history. It was addressed to a relatively small group of people rather than to an entire church. They had already been Christians for some time (5:12, 6:10). They had in the past endured persecution with confidence (10:32–35). Their community was not of the first generation of Christians, but one that had received the Gospel by tradition (2:3). On the other hand they had been taught by great teachers (13:7), and had leaders who were to be respected and imitated (13:7, 17, 24). The message in 13:24 that 'those from Italy send you greetings' suggests that they were in Italy, probably in Rome. The letter presupposes a deep knowledge of the Hebrew Scriptures and of Jewish liturgical practice, so they must have been a scholarly group, in a community that had been evangelised by converts from Judaism.

In summary, the author may well have been a teacher of a group of students who were themselves to become teachers (5:12). He was worried that they were drifting away from the faith (5:11–14). At the time he was separated from them and could not come to them in person immediately. Therefore he wrote this letter to them. It does not begin in the conventional form that Paul's letters always followed, though it ends with greetings as a letter does. It reads more like a sermon, or lecture. The author himself calls it 'a word of exhortation' (13:22).

When did he write it?

There are some indications about the time that the letter was written in what has been said already. The recipients were second-generation Christians. Their community had already suffered and survived persecution, and there are suggestions about the risk of persecutions yet to come. That indicates a time between the two persecutions of Nero in 64 CE and Domitian in about 85 CE. There is no mention of the destruction of the Temple in Jerusalem, which happened in 70 CE, but the author's argument is not based on second Temple liturgy, but on the much earlier priesthood of Melchizedek, and the Tabernacle or tent that was carried by the Israelites in the desert during their search for the promised land. Various scholars have propounded persuasive but not conclusive arguments for dates between the 60s and the late 80s, but in my humble opinion, following Brown, a date of about 80 CE would not be far wrong.

The Letter to the Hebrews is one of the two most difficult books in the New Testament for us to read and understand. (The other is the Book of Revelation.) It was written by a scholar for a group of scholars. It assumes a knowledge of the Hebrew Scriptures and of the ancient Jewish system of sacrifice that even in the author's time not all Christians would have had. It uses rabbinical methods of interpretation that are quite foreign and incomprehensible to us. Very few modern Catholics are accustomed to a detailed reading of the books of Genesis, Exodus, Leviticus, Numbers and Deuteronomy, let alone engaging in allegorical interpretation of them. Only occasionally do we have read a few selected passages from this letter in our liturgy.

Nevertheless, it is also one of the most rewarding, because of the glorious picture that it gives of Jesus Christ, in his humanity and his divinity, and his place in God's plan for our salvation.

The author ranks with Paul and John as one of the three greatest theologians of the New Testament.

The author proclaims his theme immediately in the introduction (1:1–14). In the working out of God's plan for the salvation of mankind, Jesus is superior to all that has gone before in Israel.

Jesus is superior as God's son

He proves first that Jesus is superior to the angels with seven quotations from Hebrew Scripture, including one from Psalm 45, where he has God addressing Jesus as God (1:8). Therefore we must pay attention to his message (2:1-4).

The author then introduces a theme central to the letter. Jesus, to whom all things are subject, became lower than the angels, one of us, a human being. He was crowned with glory by suffering death, so that we might become his brothers and sisters, having the one father (2:5-18).

Moses had been faithful to God, but as a servant. Jesus is greater than Moses because he was faithful as a son (3:1-6). The readers are urged to be faithful by recalling, in Psalm 95, the fate of those who followed Moses in the desert, but were not allowed to enter the Promised Land because they had lacked faith, as recorded in Numbers 14 (3:7-19). His readers are in danger of being discouraged, but this is a time of testing for them. If they wish to enter God's rest they must today be faithful, because God is able to discern our innermost thoughts and intentions (4:1-13). This passage is at first difficult to follow, because the author is using the word 'rest' in three different senses. First, there is the meaning of being at peace with God. Next, he likens that to the peace attained by those of the Israelites who finally entered the Promised Land under the leadership of Joshua. Then he alludes to God's resting on the seventh day, after the six days of creation.

Jesus is superior as High Priest

Now the author begins to develop the most characteristic concept of the letter, that of Jesus as the perfect High Priest.

The Jewish Levitical priesthood was founded by Moses at God's command after the covenant at Mount Sinai. After giving instructions for the making of the Ark of the Covenant and the Tabernacle and its furnishings (Ex 25, 26, 27), God chose Aaron and his sons to be his priests (Ex 28, 29). The three characteristics of a priest were, first, he was appointed to deal with things pertaining to God on behalf of the community. Next, he must be appointed from among the community, being completely involved in being human. Lastly he must be appointed by God. Jesus is the perfect high priest because, being the son of God, he knows God perfectly, and, as his sufferings showed, he was perfectly man, and he was appointed by God (4:14—5:10).

The writer turns again to exhortation (5:11—6:20). He reprimands his readers for their immaturity, and warns about the terrible consequences of apostasy. Nevertheless he expresses confidence that, because of their previous work and love, they have reason to hope in Jesus, since God is always faithful to his promises.

Chapter 6 of the letter ends with a reference to Jesus becoming a high priest forever according to the order of Melchizedek. There have been two previous references to Melchizedek in chapter 5. In chapter 7 the author begins to develop this idea in detail.

Who was Melchizedek?

> Melchizedek is a combination of two Hebrew words meaning king and righteousness. Salem (cf *shalom*) means peace.

Many generations before Moses was to establish the Levitical priesthood at Mount Sinai, Abram, as he then was (he was later to be renamed Abraham by God (Gen 17:5)), had settled at Hebron in the Promised Land (Gen 12:5—13:18). His nephew, Lot, was captured in a war between tribes in the Dead Sea Valley. Abram rescued Lot and defeated the attackers, much to the delight of the king of Sodom (Gen 14:1-17). King Melchizedek of Salem, described as 'priest of God most high', brought out bread and wine, and blessed Abram, who gave him one tenth of the spoils of battle (Gen 14:18-20).

This event is alluded to by the Psalmist in Psalm 110, which was taken to refer to the Messiah. Verse 1 of this psalm was quoted at 1:13, to show that Jesus was superior to the angels. Verse 4 reads, 'Yahweh has sworn an oath he will never retract. You are a priest forever of the order of Melchizedek.' Note that there is no other reference to Melchizedek in the Hebrew Scriptures, no genealogy, no hint even of where he came from or what happened to him. One of the rules of rabbinical interpretation was that if something was not mentioned in the Scriptures it did not exist. This led to a tradition that Melchizedek was eternal (7:1-3).

The Levitical priesthood, the order of Aaron, depended upon membership of the tribe of Levi. By contrast, the priesthood of Melchizedek did not. In fact Aaron's ancestor Abram had paid tithes to him, showing Melchizedek's superiority even to Abram, father of the people of Israel. Melchizedek's priesthood depended upon personal qualification, not genealogy.

The characteristics of the priesthood 'according to the order of Melchizedek' are therefore, it is that of a king, it is a priesthood of righteousness and peace, it is personal and not inherited, and it is eternal. Jesus has all these qualities. He was not of the tribe of Levi, but of Judah. His priesthood depended upon personal qualification, and God has sworn that it is eternal, as the Psalmist testified in Psalm 110:4 (7:4-17).

A new covenant

The author then develops his thesis that the change in the priesthood has brought about a change in the Law, and led to a new covenant, as foretold by the prophet Jeremiah (Jer 31:31-34). The Levitical system was not introduced by an oath of God. Priests died, they had to offer sacrifices for themselves, and they had to repeat those sacrifices endlessly and ineffectually. The priesthood of Jesus was introduced by an oath of God. Jesus is eternal, he does not have to offer sacrifice for himself, his one sacrifice of himself does not need to be repeated, and he is perfect (7:12, 18-28; 8:1-12).

The concept of a covenant, here being discussed, is central to the author's argument. It meant a right relationship between God and man. God's first covenant depended upon man's keeping the Law. When men broke the Law the covenant became ineffective. The old sacrifices were not capable of restoring the relationship, but dealt only with external regulations until the time should arrive when Christ would set things right.

The author's imagery is here influenced by his Greek philosophy. Plato's idea of reality was that there were unseen, eternal forms of things, which alone were real, whereas the world we know consists of copies of them, made of matter, marked by decay and death. The tabernacle constructed by Moses at Mount Sinai was built according to the detailed pattern dictated to him by God (Ex 25:8). Hebrews states that it was but a 'sketch and shadow' of God's throne in heaven, where Jesus is seated at the right hand (8:1-6).

This idea is elaborated in chapter 9. The author describes briefly the beauty of the Tabernacle and the Holy of Holies, into which only the high priest could enter, and that only on the Day of Atonement—*Yom Kippur*. Yet, beautiful as it was, this worship was only a copy and shadow of the real worship that only Jesus, the real high priest, can offer (9:1-14).

In the next passage the author engages in a form of argument strange and most unconvincing to us, but well known and persuasive to his readers. It is based on a pun! The Greek word *diatheke* could mean a covenant, but it could also mean a will. The death of the testator is necessary before a will comes into operation. Therefore the new covenant cannot become operative without the death of Jesus.

A basic Hebrew belief was that blood was the source of life, and that the shedding of blood was essential to sacrifice. Leviticus 17:11 reads, 'For the life of the flesh is in the blood; and I have given it to you for making atonement for your lives on the altar; for, as life, it is the blood that makes atonement.' Moses had sprinkled blood in the sacrifices that were offered after the making of the covenant at Mount Sinai. Those rites were but shadows, which could not reconcile man to God. The reality was Christ's sacrifice, in shedding his own blood in accordance with God's will. It is by God's will that his sacrifice needed to be offered only once, and was effective to remove sin (9:15-28; 10:1-18).

Words of exhortation

Consequently, the author encourages his readers; they should persevere in faith, hope and love, meeting together as a community (10:19-25). They are warned of the terrible consequences of apostasy (10:26-31), but their previous perseverance and compassion should give them endurance (10:32-39).

In chapter 11 the author puts before them a long list of figures from the Hebrew Scriptures who had demonstrated faithfulness, 'the assurance of things hoped for, the conviction of things not seen' (11:1-3).

In chapter 12 he puts before them the example of Jesus, 'the pioneer and perfecter of faith', urging them to follow him in perseverance through trials and the discipline of suffering that God administers (12:1-13). He warns them against rejecting God's grace, quoting examples from the Hebrew Scriptures (12:14-29).

As he comes to the end of his letter the author turns to practical injunctions, such as brotherly love, hospitality, sympathy for those in trouble, sexual purity and freedom from the love of money (13:1–6). His readers should remember and obey their leaders, and ignore false teachings, especially about reliance on external things such as regulations about food (13:7–17). The letter concludes with a request for prayers for the author, a beautiful conventional benediction and final greetings (13:18–23).

- *What three important things about Jesus does the Letter to the Hebrews tell us?*

Chapter 21
James

Who wrote it?

There are two questions to be answered about the authorship of this letter. First, who is the James referred to, and then, did he really write it?

In the New Testament there are references to three men named James:

James the brother of John and son of Zebedee, who was one of the original twelve Apostles (Matt 4:21), sometimes later called James the Great. He was killed by Herod in the early 40s (Acts 12:2). He could not have been the author of this letter.

James, the son of Alpheus, another of the Apostles (Matt 10:3). About him we know practically nothing. There is no suggestion that he was the author.

James who is listed as a brother of the Lord in Matt 13:55 and Mark 6:3. He was not a member of the twelve, but became prominent in the church in Jerusalem (Gal 2:9, 12; Acts 12:17; 15:13–21; 21:18). Paul calls him an apostle in the wider sense (Gal 1: 19). Josephus reported that he was executed by stoning in the early 60s. He was known from the time of Eusebius as 'James the Just'.

The letter purports to have been written by 'James, a servant of God and of the Lord Jesus Christ' and is addressed to 'the 12 tribes in the dispersion'. The author therefore was a Jewish Christian, who was interested mainly in Christians who also came from and still related to a Jewish background, and who did not live in Jerusalem. He wrote as one having authority in the church.

Such a description so obviously fitted James the Just that early tradition attributed the letter to him.

However, most modern scholars doubt that tradition. The Greek style is polished and eloquent, and the Scripture employed is from the Septuagint (Greek) version of the Hebrew Scriptures. It is unlikely that the author's mother tongue was Aramaic. For those and other reasons, most now think that the letter was probably written after James' lifetime by an unknown Christian teacher, who respected James' authority and wrote in his name, expressing some main aspects of his teaching.

It is more difficult to attribute a date to the letter with any degree of confidence. *The New Jerome Biblical Commentary* suggests that a likely date could be in the early 60s, after Paul's teaching on faith and works, but before the destruction of Jerusalem in 70 CE.

Brown notes that there is internal evidence in the letter of a developing structure in the church (3:1; 5:14–15). He considers a more likely date would be in the last third of the first century, most likely in the 80s or 90s.

> Note: I have placed it in this position in this book for mere reasons of convenience. There is no question of the development of doctrine that requires it to be placed elsewhere.

For whom was it written?

The letter was obviously not written to a particular church community, or in response to any identified crisis or problem that his readers might be experiencing. It consists of a series of exhortations, with no discernible common connection, except perhaps a concern that their faith should not be merely theoretical or abstract, but should be expressed in action and attitude in their daily lives.

The writer expected that his readers would include both rich and poor, who still identified their meeting places as synagogues (2:1–4). Many of his exhortations closely resemble the teachings of Jesus as expounded in Matthew's gospel, such as in the Sermon on the Mount (for example, compare James 1:22 and Matt 7:24; James 2:10 and Matt 5:19).

Content

This letter does not begin or end with the prayers of thanksgiving and peace so characteristic of Paul's letters. The author introduces himself as a servant of God, a title given to many religious leaders such as Moses, Abraham and the prophets in the Hebrew Scriptures. He thus indicates the source of his authority.

Particularly since Luther and the Reformation there has been a perception of conflict between Paul and James concerning Faith and Works. In Romans 3:28 Paul had proclaimed, 'A person is justified by faith apart from the works of the law' (see also Gal 2:16). At 2:24 James teaches, 'A person is justified by works and not by faith alone.'

It seems likely that James was responding, not to what Paul had actually written or preached, but to misunderstandings about what he meant.

Paul did not preach that faith alone was sufficient for salvation. He was reacting against the proposition that the observance of the ritual works prescribed by the Law of Moses, particularly circumcision, was sufficient, or needed, for his gentiles. Faith in Jesus Christ was required. He would have reacted strongly to any suggestion that such a faith did not entail consequences in the way people behave. As he said in 1 Corinthians 19, 'Circumcision is nothing and un-circumcision is nothing, but obeying the commandments of God is everything.'

When we recall that Jesus taught that all the Law and the prophets hang on the two Commandments, to love God and to love neighbour (Matt 22:38–40) it is clear that to James's statement that, 'Just as the body without the spirit is dead, so faith without works is also dead' (2:26), Paul would have responded, 'Of course'.

When Paul spoke about the insufficiency of 'works', he was referring to the ritual observances of the Law of Moses. When James spoke of 'works' he meant the practical application of Christ's law of love. There is no conflict. James would agree with Paul's 'And now faith, hope and love abide, these three; and the greatest of these is love' (1 Cor 13:13). He would simply add, 'Now put that into practice.' As he did in fact write, 'You do well if you really fulfil the royal law according to the scripture, you shall love your neighbour as yourself' (2:8).

- *This is a short letter, allowing plenty of time for deep reflection.*

Chapter 22
Titus, 1 Timothy, 2 Timothy

The Pastoral Pauline Letters

The order in which these epistles now appear in our Bibles has been determined solely by their length—the longest first, the shortest last. Their narrative sequence, the story that they assume about Paul's movements, presumes a timelapse of at least two years and travel to places of which there is no evidence apart from the letters themselves. We do not know with any degree of accuracy when they were written, nor is there any scholarly consensus that they were written by the one person who had a plan that they should be read in any particular order. I have chosen the order that I have because Titus and 1 Timothy deal with similar subject matter, while in 2 Timothy Paul is depicted contemplating his death (2 Tim 4:6-8), an appropriate note on which to conclude our consideration of the letters that bear his name

The letters purport to have been written to two of Paul's closest associates.

Paul had taken Titus, a gentile convert, with him when he and Barnabas went up to Jerusalem to persuade the leaders there about the validity of his mission, and he was not compelled to have Titus circumcised (Gal 2:1-3). Later, when Paul was having difficulty with the Corinthians, he sent Titus to them, and derived great consolation from his reports (2 Cor 2:13; 7:5-7, 13-16; 12:17-18).

Paul had encountered Timothy at Lystra, at the beginning of his second missionary journey. Timothy's mother was a Jewish convert and his father a gentile. Paul was impressed by the reports that he had of him, and persuaded him to accompany him. Because Paul knew that he would be visiting many synagogues on his mission, and people would know that Timothy's mother was Jewish, he had Timothy circumcised (Acts 16:1-3).

Timothy remained in Beroea when Paul was forced to flee to Athens (Acts 17:13-15), and then rejoined him in Corinth (Acts 18:5). He was there with Paul when Romans was written (Rom 16:21). When Paul decided to leave Ephesus to return to Jerusalem he sent Timothy ahead to Macedonia (Acts 19:21-22).

Paul later sent Timothy as his representative to Thessalonica (1 Thess 3:2, 6), to Corinth (1 Cor 4:17; 16:10-11), and probably to Philippi (Phil 2:19-23). Timothy was a co-author of four of Paul's undoubtedly genuine letters (2 Cor 1:1; Phil 1:1; 1 Thess 1:1 and Philem 1:1).

Since the letters purport to be written by Paul to associates whom he had left in charge of communities, advising them about their role as pastors of those communities, they have become known as 'the pastoral letters'.

Authorship

The letters are quite consistent with each other in style, grammatical usage and vocabulary, but they all differ markedly in each of these respects from the clearly genuine letters of Paul, more so in the cases of Titus and 1 Timothy than in 2 Timothy. The events referred to in them also are difficult to reconcile with the commonly accepted framework of Paul's life. There is much less emphasis on an imminent second coming, and there appears to be a more developed church structure than appears in the genuine Pauline letters.

Brown comments that these various factors are rarely unambiguous and produce a confusing result, so that it does not respect the evidence to profess great confidence about who wrote those epistles and when. Nevertheless he concludes that 80 to 90 percent of modern scholars would agree that they were written after Paul's lifetime, with a majority accepting the period between 80 and 100 CE as the most likely time of composition.

Brown suggests that the same author could possibly have written 1 Titus and 1 Timothy, but it is less likely that he also wrote 2 Timothy. The most likely hypothesis is that the authors were disciples of Paul or sympathetic commentators on the Pauline heritage. In the Greco-

Roman tradition it was common for a writer to seek to extend the thought of his mentor or master by saying in effect, 'The master would certainly have said such and such if faced with these particular issues', and his readers would have understood perfectly what was happening.

The authors clearly knew at least some of Paul's writings, especially Romans and 1 Corinthians, but it is not clear that they knew all of them. Nor is it clear that Paul would really have agreed with everything that they say. It is difficult, for example, to reconcile Paul's attitude to the many women he named in Romans 16 with the strictures in 1 Timothy 2:11-15. My own opinion is that a different author wrote each letter, without reference to either of the others, and that of the three the author of 2 Timothy was the most attuned to Paul's theology and successful in imitating his style.

The Letter to Titus

The letter begins with a long and formal introduction, which would hardly be needed in a letter to one who knew Paul as well as Titus did. Also, there is missing Paul's habitual prayer of thanksgiving. However, the ostensible recipient is being urged to take strong action in his community to preserve their faith, and the message is, from the beginning, invested with the authority of an apostle and servant of God. The knowledge of truth referred to stands in contrast to the false teachings later attacked in the letter.

The body of the letter may be summarised as dealing with three themes:
church structure
false teaching and
community relations and belief.

Church structure (1:5-9)

There is evidence of only one visit to Crete by Paul. That was when, on his final journey to Rome, his ship put in for a short time at Fair Havens harbour, before putting to sea again, only to be wrecked on Malta (Acts 27:7—28:1). There is no suggestion that on that occasion he engaged in any missionary activity.

The ostensible occasion for the letter is suggested to be that in a church founded by him, Paul did not himself establish a fixed structure, but he is now entrusting that task to his disciple. The practice of having elders, or presbyters, in each town was borrowed from Judaism. Their qualifications should be such as would ensure a respected leadership, faithful to sound Pauline doctrine, and able to communicate it. In the context, there does not seem to be any distinction drawn between elders (*presbuterous*, v 5) and bishops (*episkopon*, v 7).

False teaching (1:10–16)

The vitriolic attack on Cretans may indicate that the letter was not intended to be read in Crete. The quotation is from a philosopher of the sixth century BCE, Epimenides of Crete, who attacked the claim by Cretans that Zeus was dead and was buried on Crete. Cretans are here used as a type for heretical Christians, particularly those clinging to Jewish traditions, such as those declaring certain things as impure.

Community Relations and Belief (2:1–3:11)

The household code in the first part of this section (2:1-10) is reminiscent of those in Colossians 3:18—4:1 and Ephesians 5:21—6:9. In the next part (2:11—3:11) the author bases his instruction on what Christ has done for us, saving us 'not because of any works of righteousness that we had done, but according to his mercy', a sympathetic Pauline touch.

The letter ends with final messages, naming a number of fellow workers, and a blessing. Artemas and Zenas are not mentioned elsewhere in the New Testament, and we know nothing about them. Tychicus, from Asia Minor, was a companion of Paul, referred to in Acts 20:4, Colossians 4:7, Ephesians 6:21 and 2 Timothy 4:12. Apollos was the eloquent Jewish convert, who was instructed by Priscilla and Aquila in Ephesus (Acts 18:24—19:1), and who later worked with Paul in Corinth (1 Cor 4:6, 16:12). Nicopolis was probably the city in Epirus, in North Western Greece. Apart from this reference, there is no evidence that Paul ever spent any time there.

1 Timothy

In this letter, and in 2 Timothy, the opening formula includes the usual invocation of grace and peace, but also adds mercy, which is not in any of Paul's genuine letters, or in Titus.

The ostensible background is that Paul left Ephesus for Macedonia, leaving Timothy behind to preserve true doctrine among the faithful in Ephesus (1:3). He intended to return soon to Ephesus (3:14-15, 4:13). This does not accord with the accepted career of Paul and Timothy. When Paul finally left Ephesus for Macedonia, Timothy did not remain behind, but was with him when 2 Corinthians was written (2 Cor 1:1).

This letter describes Timothy as a young man (4:12, 5:1), who has a gift given 'through prophecy with the laying on of hands by the council of elders' (4:14). Nowhere in Acts or the other letters of Paul is there any reference to such a source for Timothy's authority. He is said to be subject to frequent illness for which Paul prescribes a little wine (5:23).

In the body of this letter, the author deals with the same main themes as in the letter to Titus, namely church structure, false and true teaching and community relations. However, he does not deal with them sequentially. He moves from one to the other and back again.

> Note: In this overview I have followed the same order as evolved in Titus. It is suggested that the letter be read first as a whole, and then the sections relevant to each theme.

While it is difficult to discern the actual audience addressed in Titus, it seems clear that in this letter the author was addressing the churches in and around Ephesus, where the faith had been established for some time. Enough time had elapsed for there to be a need for a procedure for dealing with complaints against elders (5:19-20).

Church structure (3:1-13; 5:3-22)

In Titus no distinction was made between elders (presbyters) and bishops (overseers). Here bishops are dealt with in one place (3:1-7) and 'elders who rule' in another (5:17-22), which would indicate that not all elders were bishops, and that bishops were ordained (5:22). The office was respected (3:1), so that they are warned not to become conceited (3:6). Much the same qualities are required for them as in Titus.

Deacons also are to have similar qualities of respectability (3:8-13). Women could be deacons (3:10), as is clear from Paul's reference to Chloe in Romans 16:1.

Widows (5:3-16) obviously constituted another special group in the church at Ephesus, although it could not be said that they held any particular office. The author seems to suggest that some elderly widows were on some sort of list, perhaps to be supported by the community, while they devoted themselves to prayer and good works. Younger widows are exhorted to look after their children or grandchildren or to remarry and raise a family.

False and true teaching (1:3–20; 3:14—4:10; 6:3–5)

It is difficult to discern whether any or what particular false teaching is being attacked. The author, as Paul, gives encouragement by his own experience of conversion through the mercy of Christ. Nothing is known about Hymenaeus or Alexander, but they are mentioned as adversaries in 2 Timothy. Handing persons over to Satan was a step in hoping for their eventual salvation (compare 1 Cor 5:4–5).

Community relations (2:1–5; 4:11—5:2; 5:24—6:2; 6:6–9)

The author begins this theme with a request for prayers for civil authorities. There are scattered instructions about the relationships between the old and the young and between men and women, on how to behave during worship, and urging respect by slaves for their masters, Christian and non-Christian.

Read literally, the instructions about women are disproportionate. There has more recently been support for a different interpretation, namely that what the author was attacking was the behaviour of some of the wealthier women in the community (2:9; 6:9, 17), or self-indulgent widows (5:6, 13), who might be influenced by false teachers with a mind for pecuniary gain (6:5). It is they who should not teach, and who are compared to Eve. There is evident in the letter a marked distrust of wealth.

In the short conclusion (6:20–21) there are none of Paul's usual greetings, but simply an exhortation to Timothy and the invocation of grace.

2 Timothy

Brown comments that the complicated debate about authorship 'should not be allowed to obscure the power of this letter read simply as it is presented: an eloquently passionate appeal of the greatest Christian apostle that his work continue beyond his death through generations of disciples'. In this commentary I have adopted the convention that the author was Paul.

Introduction (1:1–5)

The personal salutation invokes 'Grace, mercy and peace from the Father and Christ Jesus our Lord', and is followed by an eloquent prayer of thanksgiving in typical Pauline style. Timothy's family background is recalled, the reference to his mother being consistent with Acts 16:1, although his grandmother is not there mentioned. This, together with Paul's reference to the faith of his own ancestors, (1:3) links both Paul and Timothy to the faith of Israel, a link later reinforced by Paul's commendation of Scripture at 3:15–17. (To the writers of the New Testament, Scripture meant, not their own writings, but those of Israel.) This attitude fits well with Paul's letter to the Romans.

Body (1:6–4:8)

The body of the letter begins with a personal call to Timothy to renew the spiritual gifts that he has received. Note that the laying on of hands is not the community ordination ceremony contemplated in 1 Timothy 4:14. Paul alone authenticates Timothy's mission (1:6–7). Timothy is urged to rely with courage and confidence in the power of God bestowed in Christ and with the help of the Holy Spirit (1:8–14).

In a short aside Paul refers to his own situation, abandoned and in prison. We know nothing about Phygelus. Hermogenes is mentioned in an apocryphal Acts as a follower of Paul who became an apostate. Onesiphorus is named in the same source as a faithful friend of Paul, who seems here to be mourning his death (1:15–18).

Paul exhorts Timothy to be strong in faithfulness, following Christ's and his own example. The section concludes with a hymn, the first line of which recalls Romans 6:8 (2:1–13).

He then describes the characteristics that distinguish true teachers from false (2:14–26). Hymenaus is mentioned in 1 Timothy 1:20 as an opponent of Paul. We know nothing about Philetus.

In chapter 3 Paul contrasts the behaviour of false teachers with his own conduct, and exhorts Timothy to follow him and the inspired sacred writings (3:1–17). The list of vices in 3:2–5 recalls a similar list in Romans 1:29–31.

He concludes his final exhortation (4:1–8) with a moving farewell, using imagery reminiscent of Philippians 2:17; 3:12 and 1 Corinthians 9:24–25.

Conclusion (4:9–22)

There is then a relatively long and detailed closing section, referring to Paul's needs and situation, and to a number of people, some already well known to us from previous letters, others not, such as Crescens and Carpus (4:9–18).

There are greetings to Prisca and Aquila and to the household of the deceased Onesiphorus. Erastus was with Paul when he wrote Romans 16:23, and it was he who accompanied Timothy when Paul sent them ahead from Ephesus to Macedonia (Acts 19:22). Trophimus, a gentile convert from Ephesus, is mentioned in Acts as accompanying Paul and Timothy through Macedonia (Acts 20:4), and as providing the occasion for Paul's arrest in the Temple in Jerusalem (Acts 21:29). The four people named in 4:21 are not known. The final blessing is probably directed personally to Timothy, although in many manuscripts the final 'you' is plural.

Chapter 23
Luke Vol I—the Gospel according to Luke

Fig. 23.1

There is a tradition, evidenced as early as the second century, that Luke was a Syrian from Antioch, and the beloved physician who accompanied Paul on his journeys. He was not an eyewitness to the events of Jesus' life. He himself tells us that his account is based on what had been handed down by 'eyewitnesses and servants of the word' (1:1-4).

Luke is not named in the gospel. The attribution of the names of the authors to the gospels was a development of later tradition. Like all the other evangelists, he tells us nothing about himself, no doubt because he did not think that important. He wants us to focus on Jesus.

Of the four evangelists his is the most polished Greek, in which he could write in a variety of styles. He was very well read in the Septuagint version of the Hebrew Scriptures. He may have been a gentile who had converted to Judaism some time before becoming a Christian, or a Jewish convert well educated in Hellenic culture.

The result of his careful investigation of his sources is truly one work in two volumes. Volume I, the Gospel, deals with the life, death and resurrection of Jesus, while Volume II recounts the spreading of the good news from Jerusalem through Asia Minor and Greece to Rome, the centre of the then known world. The purpose of the whole work is theological, namely to expound God's plan for the salvation of humankind. In summary, Luke's description of the history of salvation, as laid out in his two volumes, is that: God's plan was foretold by the prophets and the Scriptures (24:25-27); it was realised by the life, death and resurrection of Jesus the Messiah (Acts 2:22-36); and it was being actualised throughout the Earth by witnesses empowered by the Holy Spirit (Acts 1:8).

There are three stages: Israel, Jesus and the church, Jesus is the link from Israel to the Church.

The Gospel is the longest of the four. Together with Acts, Luke's work comprises about one quarter of the New Testament. The two volumes are integrated. Luke portrays Jesus not only by telling stories in the gospel about what he said and did, but also by detailing in Acts what his followers said about him as they spread the gospel. A number of scholars have even said that a search for Luke's Christology should begin with the speeches in Acts.

Date

The majority opinion is that Luke relied on Mark as one of his sources, which indicates a date after the late 60s. The internal evidence is consistent with a date after the Roman destruction of the Temple in 70 CE (19:41–44, 21:20–24). The tradition that Luke was a companion of Paul points to a date well before 100 CE. Brown's opinion is that the best date would seem to be about 85 CE, give or take five to ten years.

Audience

Although he uses a literary technique of addressing his work to a particular reader, Theophilus, Luke was obviously writing for a much wider audience, which would have included converts from Judaism, gentiles who had been attached to a synagogue, and an increasing proportion of gentile converts. They were concerned about how God's promises made to Israel could apply to them. They were also being harassed by local synagogue leaders, as Acts makes clear. It is highly likely that they were members of churches that had been influenced by Paul's mission, in Greece or Asia Minor.

Sources

Luke acknowledges that he is basing his account on the work of others (1:1–3).
- There is Mark's gospel. About thirty-five per cent of Luke's gospel consists of material taken from Mark. Luke usually follows the same order as Mark in dealing with it, though he obviously thought that he could tell the better story. He improved the linguistic style, and omitted material that might be thought to reflect unfavourably on the Lord or the apostles, and changed the order of events sometimes to suit his own objectives.
- There is the inferred source known to scholars as 'Q', being material that is common to both Matthew and Luke but is not found in Mark. Material from this source constitutes about twenty per cent of Luke's gospel.
- The balance, not much less than half of the Gospel, is peculiar to Luke. It is difficult to tell how much Luke took from materials written by others, such as collections of hymns or of sayings of

the Lord, and how much is based on traditions particular to or composed by himself.

Finally, however, Luke has used all the materials available to him to set down an orderly account, and has organised and moulded them to fulfil his own theological purpose. The two volumes are an epic that begins in the Jerusalem Temple and ends in Imperial Rome. It includes many of the most memorable passages in all the gospels. What would Christmas be without Luke's nativity, for example, or Christianity without the parables of the prodigal son and the good Samaritan? Brown rightly comments, 'Accurately Dante described him as "the scribe of the gentleness of Christ"—more than any other Evangelist Luke has given the world a Jesus to love.'

Structure of the story

Scholars differ about the details concerning the literary structure of Luke's gospel, but the following description follows a basic structure common to most of them.

The Dedication (1:1–4)

Whether Theophilus was an actual person or not, Luke uses his dedication to him to inform the reader about his purpose. He assumes that we, like Theophilus, have already received instruction about what has been called 'the Jesus event'. He assures us that he has been careful and thorough in his investigations, that his sources are reliable, and that his book will have a structure, designed to give his story particular significance. The Greek word *asphaleia*, which is usually translated as 'truth' in v 4, (better, 'well foundedness') conveys much more than mere factual accuracy. It connotes the conviction and certainty with which we should apprehend that truth. We need reassurance, just as Theophilus did, that the promises made to Israel have been fulfilled.

Introduction—infancy and boyhood of Jesus (1:5—2:52)

The story begins in the Temple in Jerusalem, with an annunciation by an angel to Zechariah of the pending birth of John the Baptist to his wife Elizabeth. The child is to have the spirit and power of Elijah (1:5–25). According to the prophet Malachi, God was to send Elijah as his messenger before the coming Day of the Lord (Mal 3:1, 4:5). This is but the first of many links back to the Prophets and God's promises to Israel.

This annunciation is followed by another, by the same angel, Gabriel, to Mary. Her child is to be not only the Davidic Messiah (1:32–33), but the Son of God (1:35). By her faithful acquiescence Mary becomes the first disciple (1:38). She fulfils the first duty of discipleship by sharing her good news with Elizabeth. Her canticle of praise of God's mercy foreshadows her son's beatitudes, and concludes with a reference to God's promises to Israel (1:39–56).

The birth of John the Baptist is accompanied by the marvellous restoration of speech to Zechariah, who recalls God's promises to Israel, and foretells the part that his son will play in their fulfilment (1:57–80).

The birth of Jesus also is marked by the apparition of the angel who identifies him as the Messiah (2:1–20). In accordance with the Law he is circumcised and presented in the temple, where Simeon and Anna also proclaim that Jesus is the Lord's Messiah, sent for the redemption of Israel (2:21–40).

Luke then interposes a story, unique to his gospel, that demonstrates just how human and normal the growing Jesus was. Surely by the time he was twelve Mary and Joseph must have told Jesus about the circumstances of his conception, and he would have been wondering what it all might mean. With the enthusiasm typical of a 12-year-old boy, accompanied by an equally characteristic failure to contemplate consequences, he remained behind in the temple asking questions of the elders. His parents were even more puzzled than he was, but he was obedient to them when they went back to Nazareth (2:41–52).

Preparation for the ministry (3:1—4:13)

Luke places the Jesus event firmly within human history by fixing the date when the mission of John the Baptist began. The six clues place the date at about 29 CE (3:1–2). John is also clearly identified as a prophet, in the same tradition as Isaiah (3:3–6). He preaches justice and repentance, and makes clear that he is not the Messiah but the precursor. Luke does not give details of the baptism of Jesus as do the other evangelists (Mt 3:13-17, Mk 1:9-11, Jn 1:29-34), but the proclamation from on high is the same—Jesus is the son of God (3:21-22). This is the third time that Luke has stressed this message, the first being the angel's proclamation at the Annunciation (1:35), and the second the statement by the 12-year-old Jesus in the Temple (2:49).

Luke then introduces his genealogy of Jesus. It will be noted that it is quite different from that set out by Matthew (Mt 1:1-17), who traced his ancestry back to Abraham. Luke goes back to Adam and God, thus embracing all humankind (3:23-38). Satan tests this claim to be the Son of God only to be defeated by Jesus' use of the word of God in the Hebrew Scriptures (4:1-13).

Jesus' ministry in Galilee (4:14—9:50)

a. The mission begins (4:14—6:11)

Jesus returns from his retreat in the wilderness to Galilee, where he begins to preach. At his home town of Nazareth he reads in the synagogue a passage from the prophet Isaiah that identifies him as an anointed prophet. The characterisation of Jesus as a prophet is a constantly recurring theme in Luke.

In modern terminology, the word prophet is usually taken to mean someone who foretells the future. That is not an accurate description of it as it is used in the Bible. Some of the prophets did foretell the future, especially when warning the people of what would happen to them if they did not repent. But the essential meaning is that it describes one who proclaims to the people a message that God wants them to hear.

After initially receiving his message, his own people reject him, foreshadowing his ultimate fate. What particularly enraged them was his blunt message that God's mercy was not restricted to Jews, but extended also to gentiles (4:22-28).

Luke then recounts a collection of miracles and a summary of his teachings at Capernaum. He calls the first disciples and continues to manifest power by further miracles. Opposition to him from the Pharisees and the Scribes begins, grows and becomes public.

b. The Apostolic community founded and instructed (6:12—9:6)

After spending the night in prayer on a mountain, Jesus chooses a special group from among the disciples, the twelve whom he called apostles (meaning 'those who are sent out').

Prayer is given a special place in Luke. Jesus prays at each of the important turning points of his life. The revelation of his divine sonship takes place while he is praying after being baptised (3:21-22). As word about him spread he withdrew to deserted places to pray (5:16). Before choosing his apostles he spent the night in prayer (6:12-13). Peter identified him as the Messiah after he had been praying alone, with only the disciples near him (9:18-20). His transfiguration took place while he was praying (9:28-36). He prayed before teaching the disciples the Lord's prayer (11:1). He prayed that Peter's faith should not fail and that he should strengthen his brethren (22:31-34). In his agony he prayed in the garden of olives and exhorted his disciples to do so also (22:40-46). During his crucifixion he prayed for his executioners (23:34). His last words were a prayer of faith to his father (23:46).

In a scene reminiscent of Moses coming down from Mount Sinai to deliver the ten commandments to the people, Jesus comes down from the mountain where he has been communing with God in prayer and gives his new instructions, not only to Jewish people from Judaea and Jerusalem, but also to gentiles from Tyre and Sidon. He follows his instruction by word with deeds of power, first by healing the gentile centurion's servant and then by raising to life the widow's son at Naim.

Jesus answers the question conveyed to him from the imprisoned John the Baptist by pointing to the fulfilment in himself of the messianic prophecies of Isaiah (Is 26:19, 35:5-6, 42:7, 61:1). He then praises John, whom he will later place at the end of one period of history and at the beginning of another (16:16). Although John had been rejected and he himself would be rejected by some, wisdom would be vindicated by all her children, that is, John, Jesus and their disciples (7:18-35).

Women were generally marginalised in society at that time. Luke illustrates the attitude of Jesus to them by his beautiful extended story of the sinful woman forgiven because of her love and faith, and by naming some who had essential roles in his mission (7:36—8:3). At least two of them will reappear as the first witnesses to the empty tomb, bringing the news about it to the apostles (24:10).

In concluding his narrative of Jesus' instruction and formation of his apostolic community, Luke recounts his parable of the sower and his explanation of it, and the obligation on his followers to let their light shine (8:4–18). His mother and brothers arrive. Luke changes the emphasis that Mark had placed on this incident. Luke does not depict a contrast between family and discipleship. Rather the family is praised because they hear the word of God and do it. A new, extended family has been created (8:19–21).

Jesus follows his instruction by word by demonstrating his power, calming the storm, curing the gentile Gerasene and the woman with the flow of blood, and raising the daughter of Jairus from death (8:22–56). Then he gives power to the twelve, and sends them out on mission, to heal and to spread the good news, which they did with some success (9:1–6, 10).

c. End of the mission in Galilee—the turning point (9:7–50)

It is Herod who asks the question that is to be answered definitively in this turning point of Luke's story. Who is this man?

The answer begins with a demonstration of power by Jesus, in the miracle of feeding the five thousand, reminiscent of God's feeding of Israel in the desert (9:7–17). After prayer, Jesus puts the question directly to his disciples. Peter answers for them, 'the Messiah of the Lord.' Peter's answer is correct, but immediately Jesus begins to break to his disciples the news that he is not the sort of Messiah that they are imagining. He is to be rejected by the Jewish authorities, be killed and be raised again. In addition, his followers will not attain worldly power, but they will also suffer and die. To be a true follower of Christ is to take up daily the cross of suffering (9:18–27).

His followers do not yet understand that message. The question of the authority of Jesus is answered even more comprehensively in the Transfiguration, where Jesus is seen and heard talking with Moses and Elijah. In describing this scene, only Luke gives the topic of their conversation, namely 'his departure', the Greek word for which is *exodos*. Elijah had departed into heaven (2 Kgs 2:11), while Moses had led the Israelites in their departure from Egypt (the exodus). Both were significant in messianic expectation, Elijah because he was expected to return before the 'Day of the Lord' (Mal 4:5), and Moses because he predicted 'a prophet like me' to whom the people should listen' (Deut 18:15).

Peter's misguided suggestion of erecting three tents is overshadowed by the cloud, from which came the voice, 'This is my son the chosen one; listen to him' (9:33-35). This reaffirms Luke's qualification of the concept of Messiahship by adding to it Jesus' unique filial relationship with God, and the necessity that the Messiah should suffer, die and be raised, as Jesus has just told Peter and the disciples only eight days before (9:22, 28). They are ordered to listen to him, just as Moses had foretold they should.

The disciples' misunderstanding continues. They are unable to cure the epileptic boy because of their lack of faith (9:37-43). They are afraid to ask Jesus what he means by talking about his death (9:44-45). They squabble about rank among themselves (9:46-48), and they must be told that it is Jesus, not they, who will determine who can be his disciples (9:49-50). Then he sets his face to go up to Jerusalem (9:51).

Why was Jesus so determined to go up to Jerusalem? He knew that the time for his death and resurrection was approaching (9:51; 18:31-33). The phrase, 'set his face', connotes a determination to do something despite a temptation not to. Luke quotes Jesus as saying, 'I <u>must</u> be on my way, because it is impossible for a prophet to be killed outside of Jerusalem' (13:33). The next ten chapters are framed in the context of that journey. The significance of this context lies not so much in the details of the journey as in its destination.

The Journey to Jerusalem (9:51—19:44)

In these ten chapters Luke highlights his depiction of Jesus as prophet. The story is less about what Jesus did, and more about what he taught in his encounters with his disciples, the crowds and his adversaries. There are heavy demands on those who would be his disciples, and harsh criticism of those who reject him, but throughout there is an insistence on God's loving and merciful search for the repentant sinner.

There is so much that Luke wants to tell us about Jesus' teaching that it is difficult to discern any particular pattern in the parables and stories, or any meaningful relationship of any of them to any geographical place, save that the journey continues relentlessly towards Jerusalem (9:51–53; 18:31; 19:11, 28).

This section contains many parables and incidents that are unique to Luke, such as sparing the Samaritan village (9:52–56), the good Samaritan (10:29–37), Martha and Mary (10:38–42), the foolish rich man (12:16–21), the barren fig tree (13:6–9), healing the crippled woman (13:10–17), the crafty steward (16:1–8), the rich man and Lazarus (16:19–31), the widow and the unscrupulous judge (18:1–8), and Zacchaeus (19:1–10).

Jesus repeatedly confronts the Pharisees and Scribes (11:15–23, 37–52; 12:1–2; 13:14–16; 14:2–6; 16:14–15; 18:9–14). Their resentment grows (11:45, 53–54; 15:1–2; 16:14).

There are warnings to his followers about the cost of being his disciples (9:57–62; 12:4–12; 14:25–33). Yet these are balanced by his many words of encouragement (10:17–20, 23–24; 11:9–13; 12:11–12, 22–40; 18:28–30).

The centrepiece of the section, however, is the triad of parables, also unique to Luke, about the search for the one who is lost, namely, the lost sheep (15:3–7), the lost coin (15:8–10), and the prodigal son (15:11–32), which is about the father's reconciliation not only with the profligate younger son but also with the resentful elder.

Entry into Jerusalem (19:28—21:38)

After telling the parable of the nobleman, his slaves and the ten pounds, 'he went on ahead, going up to Jerusalem' (19:11–28). He entered the city riding on a colt, to the rapturous welcome of the crowds (19:29–40).

In Mark, the people welcoming Jesus into Jerusalem add the reference to Psalm 118:26, 'Blessed is the one who comes in the name of the Lord', and a Davidic, 'Blessed is the coming kingdom of our ancestor David' (Mk 11:9–10). For Luke, however, although it is a king who comes, what he brings is 'Peace in heaven and glory in the highest heaven' (19:38), which recalls the message of the angels to the shepherds at the birth of Jesus (2:14). It is not an earthly kingdom that Jesus brings to Jerusalem. He weeps because Jerusalem fails to recognise his mission and its consequences. It will rely on earthly power and not his message of peace (19:41-44). This was a classic example of the exercise by Jesus of his role as prophet. Jerusalem had not listened to the message he had brought from God, and the readers of Luke's gospel, written after the destruction of Jerusalem in 70 CE, would have recognised the truth of his prophecy.

In effect, he then took possession of the temple, driving out the money changers and preaching there every day (19:45-48). He successfully confronted the Jewish authorities who questioned his right to do those things (20:1-19), and attempted to trap him into conflict with the Roman governor (20:20-26). He silenced the Sadducees when they posed a supposed problem about resurrection (20:27-40). Luke emphasises that, as Messiah, Jesus is more than a Davidic Messiah, by his putting to the Sadducees a question based on Psalm 110:1, where David calls him Lord (20:41-44). Jesus then warned the people to beware of the false religiosity of the Scribes and the rich (20:45-47, 21:1-4).

In much of this Luke's Gospel follows those of Mark and Matthew. All three also contain an extended discourse on the future, either in or near the temple, after a disciple comments on the magnificence of the building (Mark 13:1-31, Matt 24:1-44, Luke 21:5-36).

The disciples ask when the destruction would take place, and what would be the signs that it was about to happen. Jesus does not answer that question directly. He first predicts the fall of Jerusalem and the terrors that will precede and accompany it (21:5-24). Luke's readers would recognise the accuracy of his description, as his gospel was written after those events had taken place.

He then foretells the end of the earth and his second coming (21:25-36). It is clear that he stressed that a period of time would be happening between the two—'Jerusalem would be trampled on by the Gentiles until the times of the Gentiles are fulfilled'. Instead of specifying times Jesus emphasises rather the attitudes that the disciples should adopt in any event. They should not be led astray (v 8), they are not to be afraid (v 9), and they are to rely on him for their defence when called on to testify (vv 13-15). When the end of the Earth is approaching they are not to be concerned about worldly matters, but to be on guard and to be alert (vv 34-36).

Like Paul's Thessalonians, Luke obviously expected the second coming to be soon. He would not have expected a wait of more than 2000 years. Verse 32, 'This generation shall not pass away until all these thing have been accomplished' appears also in Mark (13:30) and in Matthew (24:34), and its meaning is obscure. When Luke was writing, the generation of the apostles and disciples who had accompanied Jesus had already passed away! Luke could not have intended to report Jesus as having made a false prophecy. The reference was probably sufficiently vague for it to be repeated to enhance the sense of urgency in the whole discourse.

Betrayal, trials, passion, death and burial (21:37—23:56)

Jesus had comprehensively defeated his enemies in argument. The people flocked to hear him preaching in the temple. The Chief Priest and the Scribes therefore plotted his murder, but they had to be careful because of his popularity with the people (21:37—22:2).

At the beginning of his mission, Jesus had been tempted by Satan and had defeated him. Satan had departed 'until an opportune time' (4:1-13). That time had now arrived.

Under the influence of Satan, Judas Iscariot plotted with the authorities to betray Jesus when no crowd would be present (22:3-6).

The feast day of the Unleavened Bread arrived, preparations were made, and Jesus ate the meal with his apostles (22:7-20). Luke's description of the institution of the Eucharist substantially accords with that by Paul in 1 Corinthians 11:23-25, written perhaps some 30 years earlier.

Jesus foretells his betrayal, without identifying the traitor (22:21-23). But Judas is not the only disciple who will fail. Jesus finds it necessary to rebuke the disciples squabbling over positions of power, again emphasising that his kingdom is not an earthly one (22:24-30). He predicts that, also under Satan's influence, Peter will deny him, but that he will then repent and strengthen the others (22:31-34). The time has arrived when the scriptures predicting his shameful death must be fulfilled (22:35-38).

He then went with them to the Mount of Olives, to pray as was his custom. But first he warned the disciples that they should pray not to 'come into the time of trial', code for being tempted by Satan. He prayed for deliverance, but accepted the Father's will. Even after being strengthened by an angel, he was in agony. In his struggle against

Satan Jesus prayed more earnestly. After his agony he repeated the same warning to his disciples about temptation as before (22:39–46).

> The Greek word *agonia* is derived from another word, *agon*, which means struggle or fight.

Because at night no one was likely to be with Jesus but the disciples, Judas was able to appear with the temple police, who seized Jesus after a short but misguided attempt by one of the disciples to meet violence with violence. They took him to the High Priest's house (22:47–54).

Matthew (26:57–75) and Mark (14:53–72) tell of Peter's denial after the trial before the Council. In Luke the denial takes place on the night before the trial. Luke contrasts the behaviour of Jesus, who had prayed to be delivered from temptation, with that of Peter, who had not (22:54–62).

While waiting for daylight, those who had arrested Jesus mocked and assaulted him. They demanded that he prophesy. The reader may recall the many occasions on which he has prophesied truthfully, but, as he had said at the beginning of his ministry in Nazareth, 'No prophet is acceptable in his own country' (4:24). Ironically, the true prophet is rejected by Israel's leaders (22:63–65).

When daylight came, the Council assembled. To the Council's direct demand, 'If you are the Messiah, tell us', Jesus does not give a direct answer, but a dismissive one. He prophesies again, this time that the Son of Man would sit at the right hand of God. This response elicits their next question, 'Are you then the son of God?' His answer is just as dismissive, but just as obviously a 'yes'. The reaction of the Council shows that they accepted it as such (22:66–71).

Luke's separation of the two questions echoes the distinction in the concepts of Messiah made in the annunciation narrative (1:32, 35), and reinforces the Lukan concept that Jesus is Messiah indeed, but also related to God in a special sense, namely filial.

The assembly then took him to Pilate. They accused him of perverting the nation by forbidding the payment of taxes and saying that he was the Messiah. Lest Pilate not get the message, they added their translation of Messiah, 'a king'. The first accusation is obviously false (20:22–26). Pilate asked, 'Are you the king of the Jews?' Jesus answered dismissively, 'You say so'. Pilate must have understood that he did not claim to be a king in the earthly sense, though Luke does not disclose his reasoning. Pilate announced his decision, in effect, that he found no evidence that Jesus sought earthly power (23:1-4).

Pilate essayed a politic but unsuccessful attempt to shift responsibility by sending Jesus to Herod because he was a Galilean. Jesus silently declined to satisfy Herod's curiosity, and was sent back to Pilate (23:5-12). Pilate again repeated his finding of innocence, and tried to mollify the mob by offering a flogging, because he could not see any reason for imposing the death penalty (23:13-22).

Pilate was not a professional and impartial judicial officer, but an administrator, whose ultimate guiding principle was expediency, that is, keeping Rome happy. These were powerful people who were calling for Jesus' death, and they could cause problems for him. He acceded to their demands, and 'handed Jesus over as they wished' (23:23-25). He was able to achieve at least part of his administrative objectives, namely the deterrence of other would be messiahs, by the inscription that he ordered to be placed on the cross, 'This is the king of the Jews' (23:38). Because the Roman authorities used this messianic description of Jesus, his followers came to call him Christ from soon after the Resurrection.

As Jesus was led away to his execution, Simon of Cyrene was forced to carry the cross behind him. That the Jewish people were not united in their opposition to him is stressed by Luke's description of the great number who followed him, demonstrating their sorrow. Again Jesus foretells the destruction of Jerusalem (23:26-31).

At the place called 'the skull' Jesus and two criminals were crucified. Jesus prayed that those killing him might be forgiven. The leaders of the people derided Jesus as 'the Messiah of God, the chosen one'. The gentile soldiers mockingly used the inscription on the cross. One of the crucified criminals scoffed at him as the Messiah. They all challenged him to save himself. As Luke tells the story, the Christ, who could have but did not save himself, by his death and resurrection saved us.

In Matthew (27:44) and Mark (15:32), both the criminals join in the derision. But Luke has a point to make. One of the criminals does not mock. Nor does he seek salvation. He confesses his crime. He does not seek to avoid the consequences of it. He knows that they are both about to die. All he asks is that Jesus remember him when he comes into his kingdom. This is a recognition that Jesus is a Messiah, but of a different kind, one whose kingdom is not of this world. It is also an example to us of what is involved in true repentance and of Jesus' will to forgive anyone who seeks his forgiveness. It is a crucified criminal who is the first to be told explicitly, by his saviour, that his faith in the crucified Christ is to be rewarded by entry that day into paradise (23:32–43).

It fell dark at noon, and at three in the afternoon the curtain of the Temple was torn in two, signifying the end of God's former ways with Israel. Jesus commended his spirit to his Father and died. The representative of earthly power, the centurion, confirmed Pilate's concession that Jesus was not the kind of messiah who could be a danger to Roman power. He was innocent.

The crowd dispersed, watched by his disciples. Luke mentions specifically the women who had followed Jesus from Galilee (23:44–49).

Luke continues to stress that not all the Jewish people, or even all its leaders, were responsible for the death of Jesus. Joseph of Arimathea was a member of the Council, who had not agreed to their plans. He asked for the body, and gave it a proper interment, in a tomb instead of a common and unmarked grave usual for executed criminals. The women watched, and returned to prepare spices and ointments. They then observed the Sabbath.

> Note: As Brown writes, from one end of his life to the other Jesus has lived within the confines of Judaism (23:50–56).

Mary Magdalen, Mary the mother of James, Joanna and others with them had seen where Jesus was entombed, and they returned on the morning after the Sabbath to finish the task of anointing the body. They found the stone rolled back, and the tomb empty. Two angels appeared to tell them that Jesus had risen. They reminded the women that Jesus had foretold his death and resurrection. The women remembered his words and went and told the Apostles, who ridiculed their story and did not believe them. It is the women who bring the message of salvation only to be disbelieved by the men. Even Peter, who at least ran to the tomb to check the evidence, simply returned home amazed. The men needed more than an empty tomb on which to build their faith.

Unlike Matthew (Matt 28:7), and Mark (16:7), Luke makes no mention of a return to Galilee. For him, the story that began in Jerusalem, the centre of Judaism, would end there (24:1–12).

In the story, unique to Luke, about Jesus' appearance to the two disciples walking on the road to Emmaus, Luke sums up the point that he has been making throughout his gospel. They tell the stranger whom they meet on the way that they had hoped that Jesus might be the one to redeem Israel, but their hope had been shattered by the crucifixion and death. This is the major difficulty faced by the disciples, and dealing with it is a central concern for Luke. The stranger then gave an exegesis of the scriptures, to make the point that it was 'necessary that the Messiah should suffer these things and then enter into his glory.'

They persuaded the stranger to join them at the inn. After his exposition of Scripture, they recognised him in the breaking of bread. As they recognised him he vanished. The Christian community was to follow this pattern in their liturgy. We no longer have Jesus physically with us, but we experience him in scripture and sacrament. They hurried back to Jerusalem to find that the disciples also had a story to share with them, that the Lord had indeed risen and appeared to Simon.

It is while they were talking about this that Jesus appeared. Despite his greeting of peace they were startled. Jesus demonstrated to them that he was not a ghost by showing his wounds and eating some fish. The disciples had mixed emotions, joy, wonder, and yet still some disbelief.

Again Luke has Jesus repeat that central theme of his Gospel, namely that Jesus' death and resurrection had been part of God's plan, foretold in the Scriptures, to which Jesus opened their minds. However, he now added that it was also part of that plan that repentance and forgiveness is to be proclaimed to all humankind. Luke's Volume II will describe the beginnings of that proclamation. The disciples are to be witnesses to God's plan, but it would be beyond their abilities as they are. Jesus commands them to stay in Jerusalem until God fulfils his promise and sends them the power they will need (24:13–49).

The Ascension (24:50–53)

He led them out as far as Bethany, and while blessing them ascended into heaven. Again, Luke's characterisation of Jesus as prophet is reinforced by the parallel with the ascension of Elijah and his promise of a share in his spirit to his disciple Elisha (2 Kgs 2:1–18). The disciples returned joyfully to Jerusalem, to praise God in the temple. The story ends where it began, in the temple (24:50–53).

- *What three important things does Luke tell us about Jesus in his Gospel?*

Chapter 24
Luke Vol II—the Acts of the Apostles

Scholars agree that the author of Luke's gospel also wrote Acts. There is no evidence of how much later he wrote it, so that a time in the late 80s seems likely. That would place its writing over fifty years after the Ascension, and about 20 years after the death of Paul.

As with the Gospel, Acts was addressed to people already Christian, not to convert, but to confirm. It was meant to address concerns raised by the persistent rejection of the gospel by Jewish authorities and audiences, and the growth of a gentile membership, alienated from Israel as the biblical people to whom the promises were made. The principal argument of the two works is the continuity of salvation history through the life of Jesus detailed in the Gospel, and the beginnings of the church recorded in Acts.

A convenient overview of the structure of Acts is as follows.

1		Introduction to the era of the church	1:1—2:13
2		Mission of the church in Jerusalem	2:14—8:3
	a	Appeals to Israel	2:14—3:26
	b	Tribulations of the early church	4:1—8:3
3		Missions in Samaria, Judea and Syria	8:4—12:25
	a	Philip in Samaria	8:4-40
	b	Conversion of Saul	9:1-3
	c	Peter leads the church	9:32—11:18
	d	Antioch and Jerusalem	11:19—12:25
4		Barnabas and Saul on mission and Council of Jerusalem	13:1—15:35
5		Paul's path to the ends of the earth	15:36—28:31

    a Paul's major missions   15:36—20:38
    b Paul as prisoner in Palestine   21:1—26:32
    c Paul's final journey, to Rome   27:1—28:31

1 Introduction to the era of the church

Ascension (1:1–11)

The dramatic last chapter of the gospel began at early dawn on the first day of the week (24:1), with the discovery of the empty tomb. That same day (24:13), Jesus appeared to the two disciples on the way to Emmaus and disappeared from their sight. That same hour (24:33) they got up and returned to Jerusalem to tell the disciples. While they were still talking (24:36) Jesus appeared and spoke and ate with them. Then he led them out to Bethany and was lifted up. That all appears to have happened in the space of one day.

Acts does not merely take up the story from that point. Luke recapitulates, briefly summarising what the Gospel had been about. He then tells us that after his suffering, Jesus had been appearing to the disciples during 40 days (1:3)!

This illustrates that Luke is not writing history in the modern sense, where accurate dates and times are of the essence. His stories are based on real events, but if changing a date helps him to make an important theological point, he could place the event in a temporal context that helped him to emphasise that point.

Here the period of forty days is significant. It allows sufficient time for the preparation of the disciples for their empowerment to undertake their mission. There were precedents. Moses spent 40 days and 40 nights on the mountain before God gave him the two tablets of the covenant (Ex 24:18, 31:18, 34:28). The spies sent by Moses into Canaan returned after 40 days with their report (Num 13:25). For their faithlessness the Lord condemned the Israelites to 40 years in the wilderness, a year for every such day (Num 14:32-34). Elijah spent 40 days and 40 nights on his journey to Horeb to receive the Lord's instructions (1 Kgs 19:8-18). Jesus was tempted in the desert for 40 days before he began his preaching (Luke 4:1, 14, 15).

By the overlap Luke is stressing continuity between the life of Jesus and the life of the church as being parts of the one message of salvation.

Although Jesus had been with them for 40 days, with many convincing proofs, the apostles still had their minds set on the restoration of the kingdom to Israel. At Mount Olivet Jesus told them that they did not need to know the times when the father would do whatever it was he had decided. They were to receive power from the Holy Spirit, and to be his witnesses to the ends of the earth. With that he was lifted up out of their sight, and two angels appeared, telling them that Jesus would return just as he had left.

Disciples prepare (1:12–26)

Luke names the 11 remaining of the chosen twelve, who returned the short distance to a room in the city, where they were joined in prayer by certain women, including Mary the mother of Jesus. The group numbered about 120 persons.

Mary was the central figure in the first two chapters of Luke's gospel. She reappears in the first chapter of Acts.

Peter described the death of Judas Iscariot, and asked that another who had been with Jesus during the whole of his ministry be chosen to bear witness to the resurrection. Mathias was chosen by lot, but does not figure again in the New Testament. It was simply important that the original witnesses to the resurrection should be 12 in number, to show continuity of the Church with the 12 tribes of Israel.

The term apostle is not restricted to the twelve, though it included them. The twelve formed an irreplaceable symbol, but were not to become part of the administrative structure of the Church. When James the brother of John was killed by King Herod, he was not replaced (12:2). The apostles formed a wider group, who were to found church communities and spread the gospel. Paul was to become an apostle in this sense, and in Galatians insisted firmly on his right to be so designated (Gal 1:15–17). He even described his relatives Andronicus and Junia as 'prominent among the apostles' (Rom 16:7).

Pentecost (2:1–13)

When the day of Pentecost had come the Holy Spirit descended on all of those gathered in the house, and they began to speak in other languages.

Pentecost (from the Greek word for 50), was the name given to the Jewish Feast of Weeks, because it was celebrated 50 days or seven weeks after Passover. The interval between the two feasts was roughly the same as that between the exodus of the people out of Egypt (Passover) and the receipt by Moses of the covenant at Mount Sinai, when the Israelites became God's people.

At the sound of the mighty wind which accompanied the appearance of the tongues of fire, a crowd of people then in Jerusalem gathered, and each was astonished to hear the Apostles speaking in their own language. The countries from which they came, listed by Luke, covered the whole of the Eastern Empire to Rome itself. Luke indicates the reach of the evangelising that is about to begin, by which people from all nations will become God's people.

Fig. 24.1
Pentecost—Duccio di Buoninsgna (1308); Museo dell'Opera del Duomo, Siena.

2 Mission of the church in Jerusalem 2:14—8:1a
Appeals to Israel (2:14—3:26)

Peter immediately assumed leadership. Addressing 'Men of Judea and all who live in Jerusalem' he claimed that the marvel that they had heard, of the disciples speaking in tongues, was a fulfilment of the prophecy of Joel, that on the Lord's Day God would pour out his spirit upon all who would prophesy.

Then speaking to 'You who are Israelites', he proclaimed that Jesus, attested to them by God by works of power, had been handed over to them according to the plan of God, and crucified by the Romans, but raised from death by God, fulfilling the prophecies of David. God had made Jesus, whom they had crucified, both Lord and Messiah. The sequel was that three thousand were baptised. The disciples prayed and ate together, and shared their possessions with the needy, as the result of which their numbers grew (2:14-47).

After curing the man who had been lame from birth in the portico of the Temple, Peter again addressed the Israelites. He charged them with handing over Jesus, the holy and righteous one, to Pilate, to be killed. 'You killed the author of life, whom God raised from the dead. To this we are witnesses.' The lame man had been cured in his name. The Israelites had acted in ignorance, but God had fulfilled the prophecies that the Messiah would suffer. He called on them to repent, and quoted Moses' prophecy that God would raise up from their people a prophet like himself, to be obeyed. They were the descendants of the prophets and the covenant with Abraham, and so God had sent Jesus first to them (3:1-26).

Tribulations of the early church (4:1—8:1(a))

The result of this speech was that five thousand were converted, but Peter and John were arrested. Brought the next day before the high priest and the elders and rulers, Peter proclaimed that the lame man had been cured by the name of Jesus, whom they had crucified, and whom God had raised from the dead. Peter and John were ordered not to speak in the name of Jesus. They refused to obey, and were threatened, but allowed to go free. When their friends heard of their release, they glorified God and prayed that they might continue to speak God's word with boldness. The Spirit came upon them all (4:1-31).

The believers became a united group, selling their possessions so that the proceeds could be distributed to all in need. Two of them, however, Ananias and his wife Sapphira, pretended to be donating all the proceeds of sale of a piece of property, when they were only giving part. Peter saw through their deception, and they both died suddenly, bringing great fear to the Church. The apostles continued to heal many sick and afflicted, and they were held in high esteem by the people. Great numbers of men and women became believers (5:1-16).

Because they were continuing to attract followers, the high priest had Peter and John imprisoned again, but they escaped with the miraculous help of an angel, and were again brought peacefully before the council. Challenged for their disobedience, Peter answered that they had to obey God rather than human authority. He proclaimed to them that God had raised up Jesus, whom they had crucified, and who had been sent to bring repentance and forgiveness of sins.

When the Council heard this they were enraged and wanted to kill them, but were dissuaded from this by Gamaliel. They merely had them flogged and ordered them again not to speak in Jesus' name. They rejoiced that they were considered worthy to suffer for doing so (5:17-42).

The common theme in all these speeches is, first, that they were made by Peter. Jesus' prayer is fulfilled, that Peter would not fail and would turn and strengthen his brethren (Lk 22:31-32). Second, they demonstrate that from its earliest beginnings, the fundamental message of the Church was that Jesus had been killed, but had been raised, proving that he was the Messiah promised by the prophets, and the Son of God, and that the message that he brought was one of repentance and forgiveness.

For a short time active persecution by the authorities died down, but internal tensions arose in the community, between those who had been brought up as Jews, who spoke Aramaic or Hebrew ('the Hebrews'), and Jews or pagan converts who were acculturated to the Greco-Roman civilisation, and who spoke mainly Greek ('the Hellenists'). The twelve made it clear that they wished to concentrate on prayer and spreading the word of God, and proposed that the community choose seven suitable men to undertake the material task of distributing food fairly. Stephen and six others were chosen and the apostles prayed over them and laid hands on them (6:1–7).

Stephen, however, did not restrict himself to menial tasks. He did not worship in the temple, as did the twelve, but belonged to a synagogue of Jews from places other than Jerusalem. There he proclaimed the good news, which led to arguments with other members. Being full of grace and power, he usually won. Those who lost the arguments were resentful, and in revenge stirred up the people with false allegations of blasphemy, so that he was arrested and brought before the council.

In what follows, Luke draws many parallels between Stephen and Jesus. He was full of grace and power, and did great wonders and signs. He spoke with wisdom and the spirit. When brought before the Council his face shone like an angel, as did that of the prophet Moses (Ex 35:29, 30, 35). As a prophet he was rejected and killed. As he died he prayed for forgiveness for his killers.

The charges brought against Stephen were obviously false. Jesus had never said that it would be he who would destroy the temple. He did not seek to change the customs handed down by Moses. He said that he came to fulfil the Law not to destroy it. But Stephen did not respond by a simple denial. He reduced the charges to absurdity by giving a detailed description of God's plan for Israel and the rejection of that plan by his accusers.

There was no preserved transcript of the trial or of Stephen's speech, and Luke was not there. Undoubtedly Stephen would have said something, and the general purport of that may well have been handed down by the tradition on which Luke relied. But the speech as reported by Luke is a Lucan construct, designed to emphasise a theological point that he wished to make, a technique quite common in the literature of the time and well understood by his readers (6:8–15).

This speech is the longest of all those in Acts. Luke obviously regarded its content as being particularly important. Although it is long and a little complicated, it is worthy of careful reading. It also marks the time at which the Church ceased to be confined to Jerusalem, and began to spread to other cities.

Stephen began politely enough. He embarked upon a summary of the history of the relationship between God and the Jewish people, of whom he claimed to be a member. His summary did not follow exactly the stories as told in Genesis and Exodus, but the differences need not concern us at this stage.

> Note: As you read Stephen's stories of Abraham, Joseph and Moses notice his emphasis on the part played by God in guiding Israel's history. The history is one of prophecy and fulfilment.

At the end of the speech came the counter charges. Every lawyer with any experience knows that it is seldom useful for an accused person to attack the tribunal. Nevertheless that is the brave task that Stephen embarked upon. He accused those listening to him that they and their ancestors had stubbornly refused to accept the messages sent by God through his prophets, especially Moses, and they now refused to accept that Jesus was the Messiah promised and prefigured in Israel's history. They had rejected and killed him. They persisted in their adherence to the temple worship as the fulfilment of God's promises, when in fact that fulfilment was Jesus Christ.

His listeners became enraged. Stephen proclaimed that he had a vision of Christ standing at the right hand of God. At that, without any pretence of a lawful trial or sentence, they dragged him out of the city and stoned him to death. As he was being stoned, just as Jesus had done (Lk 23:34, 46), he commended his spirit to God and prayed for his murderers (7:1–60).

Some devout men buried Stephen. The authorities then embarked upon a severe persecution of the church, so that all except the Apostles scattered throughout Judaea and Samaria. Saul, who had been present at the stoning of Stephen and approved of it, took part enthusiastically, committing men and women to prison (8:1-3).

3 Missions in Samaria, Judea and Syria (8:1(b)—12:25)

> For the following sections it will be beneficial to refer to the maps on pages 4, 8, 12 and 13.

Philip in Samaria

The apostles still worshipped in the temple, whereas Stephen had minimised its place in salvation history, so that it was probably the Hellenists who were forced to flee Jerusalem while the Apostles were able to stay. It seems that Philip was Stephen's successor amongst them. He went to Samaria, where the people did not accept the Temple in Jerusalem as the only place of worship. There he was received eagerly, converting even the prominent magician, Simon and his followers.

The apostles sent Peter and John to bring the Holy Spirit to them. Simon offered them money to be able to exercise their powers of healing, (whence the term 'simony' is derived). Peter offered him instead the opportunity to repent. On their way back to Jerusalem they also preached the word in Samaria (8:4-25).

Philip was guided to meet a nobleman from Africa, who had been to worship in Jerusalem, and who was trying to understand the prophecies of Isaiah while he travelled in southern Judaea. Just as Jesus had (Lk 24:27, 44-45), Philip was able to interpret the Scriptures for him and to tell him the good news about Jesus. Although Jewish law would not permit a eunuch to be accepted as a Jewish convert, Philip baptised him into the new Israel, the church (8:26-40). Philip was transported miraculously to another town in Judaea, and made his way north to Caesarea, proclaiming the good news to all the towns he came to on the way.

Conversion of Saul (9:1-31)

Luke will depict Paul as telling his own story of his conversion in his speeches later in Acts, to the people in Jerusalem after his arrest (22:3-21), and to Agrippa on his way to Rome (26:2-23). Those versions are consistent with Luke's account (9:1-19), and with each other, but they do not match exactly what Paul himself had written in his letter to the Galatians (Gal 1:13-24). Paul's version in his letter is the more likely to be closer to the historical facts, but Luke has shortened the time frame of events for dramatic effect. He depicts Saul as preaching enthusiastically in Damascus immediately after he had been converted and regained his sight. In both versions, however, after some time in Damascus he went to Jerusalem, though in Acts his departure from Damascus was somewhat more dramatic. In both versions also he joins up with Barnabas. After another dramatic escape from those who wanted to kill him, he leaves the scene for a short time, returning to his home town, Tarsus. The church spread and was at peace in the whole of Palestine (9:20–31). The scene shifts back to Peter, no doubt to show that he and Saul were preaching the same gospel, but also to give proper precedence to Peter.

Peter leads the church (9:32—11:18)

Luke now addresses the two major problems that confronted the early church, and it is Peter who is guided by the Spirit to proclaim the solutions. The problems are, firstly, whether converts should be required to observe the prescriptions of Judaism about food and consorting with gentiles, and secondly, whether gentile converts should be circumcised. The real issue was whether being or becoming a Jew was more important for salvation than faith in Jesus Christ.

Peter's authority is first established by a series of miracles that recall significant miracles performed by Jesus. He heals the paralytic Aeneas in the name of Jesus Christ (9:32–35), recalling the cure by Jesus of the paralysed man in Luke 5:24–26. He raises Tabitha from the dead (9:36–43) as Jesus had raised the daughter of Jairus in Luke 8:49–50.

There follows a long and detailed story about a vision seen by Peter in which he was told three times that foods traditionally held to be unclean are not unclean. He travelled to Caesarea with men who had been sent to fetch him by a God-fearing centurion, Cornelius, after a dream. Cornelius told Peter about his dream. Peter informed him and his gentile companions that God had shown him that he should not call anything unclean, and that it was therefore not unlawful for him to associate with gentiles.

Peter preached to them that God shows no partiality, and told them about the coming of Jesus Christ, with his message of peace, and about his crucifixion and resurrection. While he was speaking the Spirit descended on all his audience, who began speaking in tongues. This divine intervention demonstrated that gentiles also could receive the Spirit. Peter ordered them to be baptised in the name of Jesus Christ (10:1–48).

When Peter returned to Judaea he was criticised for having eaten with uncircumcised men. Luke then has Peter recount in detail his dream, his journey to Caesarea, Cornelius's dream, and the coming of the Spirit on the gentile audience. His critics were silenced, and accepted that God had given salvation even to gentiles (11:1-18). By his repetition of detail Luke shows how important this message is.

Antioch and Jerusalem

The Jewish Christians who had been scattered after the death of Stephen spread through Asia Minor and to Antioch, where they preached only to Jews. Others arrived from Cyprus and Cyrene and converted many gentiles. News of this travelled to Jerusalem, and Barnabas was dispatched to Antioch. Impressed by what he saw, he went to find Saul and brought him back to Antioch, where they preached for a year. It was in Antioch that the followers of Jesus became known as Christians (11:19-26).

When a widespread famine occurred during the reign of Claudius, as foretold by the prophet Agabus, the disciples sent relief to the church in Jerusalem by Paul and Barnabas (11:27-30).

> Some quite good ancient manuscripts say they returned 'to' Jerusalem, and that is the translation in NRSV, but those that say 'from' make more sense.

In Jerusalem King Herod began a persecution. He had James the brother of John executed. Then he had Peter imprisoned. Peter was delivered from prison by an angel. Herod executed the guards. Peter went to Caesarea (12:1-19). King Herod died a disgusting death after having been hailed as a God. Having completed their mission in Jerusalem, Saul and Barnabas returned to Antioch, taking with them John Mark (12:20-25).

4 Barnabas and Paul on mission, and the Council of Jerusalem (13:1—15:35)

The teachers and prophets at Antioch, inspired by the Holy Spirit, prayed and laid hands on Barnabas and Saul and sent them off on their mission (13:1-3).

They went first to Seleucia, a port town a short distance from Antioch. From there they sailed to Cyprus, landed at Salamis and preached from there to Paphos at the far end of the island. At Paphos Paul confronted a false Jewish magician, who became blind, leading the proconsul to be converted. In this passage Luke informs us that Saul was also known as Paul, and he is referred to as Paul in the rest of the book (13:4–12).

From Paphos they sailed to Perga, a port on the southern coast of what is now Turkey, but was then called Pamphilia. There John Mark decided to return to Jerusalem, a decision which we will later find upset Paul considerably. Barnabas and Paul journeyed a bit more than 150 km north to a city called Antioch in Pisidia, to distinguish it from the much more important city of Antioch in Syria.

While in the synagogue there Paul was invited to speak to the people. Luke then sets out in detail a long speech in which Paul outlines the history of the Jewish people, the descent from David of Jesus the saviour, the preaching of John the Baptist, the death and resurrection of Jesus, and the good news of salvation through him promised to the Jewish people. The speech is in harmony with those given by Peter, and its length and detail emphasise the importance that Luke places upon its message.

The speech was well received, and on the next Sabbath there was a large crowd to hear Paul, which aroused the jealousy of the Jewish authorities, who argued with him. Paul and Barnabas announced that since the Jewish authorities had rejected the good news, which had been delivered first to Israel, they would turn to the gentiles. The gentiles were glad to hear this and many believed. The authorities stirred up a persecution and drove Paul and Barnabas out of the city. They travelled a little over 100 km east to Iconium (13:13–13:52).

Despite what they had said in Antioch of Pisidia, Paul and Barnabas preached first in the synagogue at Iconium. Again many Jews and gentiles were converted, but some unbelieving Jews stirred up trouble against them. Although they remained there for some time, eventually they were forced to flee to Lystra, just south of Iconium.

Here Paul cured a man who had been crippled from birth, showing that Paul had received the healing power of Jesus in dealing with the gentiles just as Peter had done in dealing with the Jews. This miracle caused the pagan inhabitants to think that Paul and Barnabas were gods, and to prepare to offer sacrifice to them. Hostile Jews from Antioch and Iconium caused them to be stoned, almost killing Paul. He recovered the next day, and they fled to Derbe, 150 km to the south-east.

After they had made many disciples in that region, Paul and Barnabas retraced their steps, encouraging their converts and appointing elders to lead them as they went. Eventually they sailed back to Antioch, where they reported to the church all that had happened to them (14:1—14:28). This ended what has conventionally been called Paul's first missionary journey.

Paul and Barnabas in their mission had created churches largely made up of gentiles. Christianity was becoming a largely gentile religion, separate from Judaism. There were those in Jerusalem who had not been convinced by Peter's encounter with Cornelius. They became alarmed and sent men to Antioch to preach the need for circumcision.

The resulting conflict moved the church in Antioch to send Paul and Barnabas and some others up to Jerusalem to discuss the problem with the apostles and elders. It is at first sight difficult to reconcile the version of events in Acts with what Paul had written in Galatians 2:1-10. Perhaps Paul, defending his role as an apostle, was moved to stress his part in what happened more than Luke needed to.

Be that as it may, Paul and Barnabas went up to Jerusalem with the news that the Spirit had demonstrated that circumcision was not necessary. After a debate, in which Luke reports Peter and James, but not Paul or his opponents, that question was settled, and the elders sent Paul and Barnabas and some others back to Antioch with a letter to that effect, but including an admonition to refrain from food that had been offered to idols and other practices associated with idolatry (15:1-35). Christians no longer had to become Jews to be saved, but the questions of the food laws and eating with gentiles remained as a source of conflict, as Galatians 2:11-16 demonstrates.

> Note: Read again what is written in chapter 7—Galations, where this mattter is dealt with in more detail.

5 Paul's path to the ends of the earth (15:36—28:31)

Practically the whole of the rest of Acts is taken up with Paul. There are varying conventions about the numbering of his journeys as depicted in Acts, but any system could be misleading, as it is apparent from his letters that he visited many more places than are referred to by Luke. Instead of numbering them I have simply described them.

Acts does not refer to the confrontation between Paul and Peter about eating with gentiles, recounted in Galatians 2:11-14. Think how disappointed Paul must have been when views that he held so strongly about the unity of the church, especially at the Eucharist, were not shared by Peter or even Barnabas, after all they had been through. Then when Barnabas wanted John Mark, who had turned back from their first journey, to accompany them on further mission, his anger and disappointment flared up. He and Barnabas parted company. Barnabas and John Mark went to Cyprus, and we read nothing more about them in Acts. To accompany him on his next journey Paul chose Silas, who had helped bring the message to Antioch from the Council of Jerusalem.

From Antioch, through Asia Minor to Greece and return to Jerusalem

They travelled north, through Syria and Paul's home country, Cilicia, strengthening the churches as they went (15:36–41).

They then went westward to Derbe and Lystra, where Paul encountered Timothy, of whom he heard good reports. He persuaded Timothy to join him. Because Timothy had a Jewish mother, Paul persuaded him to be circumcised, so that there would be no controversies whenever they visited a synagogue, or, especially, the Temple in Jerusalem. They went from town to town, bringing with them news of the decision of the elders in Jerusalem that gentiles did not need to become Jews in order to be Christians (16: 1–5).

They continued westwards, through what is now Turkey, ultimately arriving at Troas, on the western coast. There Paul had a vision of a man calling him to come to Macedonia, a name then given to what now includes the northern part of Greece.

Philippi

Here the form of the narrative changes to 'we', perhaps indicating that Luke accompanied Paul and Timothy on this part of their mission, or that he was quoting from a diary kept by an anonymous companion. They sailed to Greece, arriving at Neapolis, the port city of Philippi, a leading city of the district. It appears from his letters that his stay in Philippi 'for some days' was in fact quite a long stay. There was no synagogue in this city, so they went to a place of prayer by the river outside the gates. There he met and baptised Lydia and her household. She was a woman who dealt in valuable purple cloth, and so was probably quite wealthy. Although Paul usually liked to live independently, Lydia had obviously a forceful personality, because she prevailed upon Paul to stay in her home (16:6–15).

Paul drove out a spirit of divination from a slave girl who was bringing attention to them, which annoyed her owners because they could no longer make money from her. They dragged Paul and Silas before the magistrates, who had them stripped, flogged and imprisoned. An earthquake freed them, terrifying the jailer, who was so relieved to see that they had not escaped that he took them to his home and fed them, and he and his household were converted. When the magistrates sent a message that Paul and Silas were to be freed, Paul declared his Roman citizenship forcing the magistrates to apologise. He and Silas went back to Lydia's house for a time before departing. Paul's deliverance from prison, reminiscent of Peter's escape, shows that God is with his apostle in his mission to this superstitious pagan world (16:16—16:40).

Thessalonica

Paul and Silas then went westward through Amphipolis and Apollonia, to Thessalonica, a city with a sufficient number of Jewish inhabitants to have its own synagogue. It is today the second-largest city in Greece. Perhaps the anonymous companion remained behind in Philippi until Paul should return.

On three Sabbaths Paul went to the synagogue, as was his custom, and preached about the death and resurrection of Jesus, the Messiah. A good number became believers, but those who did not engineered a riot. The mob attacked the house of Jason, where Paul and Silas had been guests, and dragged Jason before the magistrates. Paul and Silas were sent off to Beroea, a city on the east coast of Greece, a short distance south-west from Thessalonica. The Jews in the synagogue there were more welcoming than those in Thessalonica.

Nevertheless the hostile Jews from Thessalonica pursued them and stirred up the crowds in Beroea. Paul was sent south to Athens, leaving Timothy and Silas behind, with instructions to join him as soon as possible (17:1–15).

Athens

Rome may have been the centre from which the world was ruled, but the centre of art and philosophy was Athens. It was, of course, filled with beautiful buildings and statues, most of which were devoted to idolatry. Paul engaged in discussions, and was eventually brought to the Areopagus, The Hill of Mars, where the Greek philosophers and leaders gathered.

Think what an opportunity this must have seemed to Paul. He was sure of his message. He was well versed in Greek and in Greco-Roman oratory. His speech as reported in Acts is, of course, a Lukan construction, but it was based on the tradition of what Paul did say, and we can be sure that Paul was as eloquent as Luke makes him out to be.

Yet his presentation failed miserably. The wise philosophers were unable to entertain the concept of a man rising from the dead. He obtained only a few converts, and decided to go on to Corinth. In the letter he wrote later to his Corinthian converts we can read the effect that this episode had on him and his theology.

> Read again 1 Cor. 1:17 to 2:5, and see how he abjures mere human wisdom. He had learned his lesson in Athens (17:16–17:32).

Corinth

In Corinth he met two Jewish converts, refugees from Rome, Aquila and Priscilla. (In his letters Paul was to refer to her as Prisca.) They were of the same trade as he was, tent makers, and they were to become significant co-workers with him in his later career, as his letters testify. They were to return to Rome, where Paul expected to meet them when he planned to travel to Rome (Rom 16:3). Silas and Timothy arrived from Macedonia.

The hostile Jews tried to have Paul punished by the Roman proconsul, Gallio, who refused to become involved in religious arguments. The date of Gallio's service in Corinth is available from other sources, and this reference is important in dating Paul's activities (18:1–17).

Also, while in Corinth, Paul wrote his first letter, to the Thessalonians.

Corinth to Ephesus

After some considerable time in Corinth, Paul returned to Antioch in Syria. On the way he left Priscilla and Aquila in Ephesus, and visited Jerusalem. He then made another journey into Galatia and Phrygia (18:18–23).

Acts then shortly introduces Apollos, an enthusiastic convert, who benefits from further instruction from the husband-and-wife team of Aquila and Priscilla (18:24–28).

Paul next appears in Ephesus, where some disciples received the Holy Spirit. Paul was able to preach in the synagogue there for three months, before some of the Jews there forced him to change his venue to a lecture hall in the city. There he continued to preach for a further two years, working many miracles. Also while he was there a riot broke out, fomented by the silversmiths who traded in silver shrines of the goddess Artemis (19:1–41).

Ephesus to Macedonia, Greece and Miletus

After the riot, Paul left for Macedonia and Greece, returning to Troas, where he raised from the dead a young man who was overcome by the length of his sermon (20:1–12). From Troas he sailed down the west coast of present-day Turkey to Miletus. There he made an emotional farewell to the elders from Ephesus (20:13–38).

Paul as prisoner in Palestine

From Miletus Paul sailed to Tyre, on the coast of Palestine. After a short stay there he sailed south to Caesarea, where he encountered a prophet who foretold his imprisonment (21:1–14). He then proceeded up to Jerusalem, where he and the elders exchanged news about the spread of the gospel.

It is obvious that the elders had heard misleading reports about what exactly Paul had been teaching, so he undertook a period of purification in the temple to show his loyalty to Judaism. That led only to a riot in the temple, during which he was seized, to be rescued by the Roman soldiers.

The Tribune in charge of the soldiers allowed him to address the crowd, which he did in Hebrew, telling once again the story of his conversion. After being quiet for a time the crowd again began demonstrating. The Tribune ordered Paul to be taken into the barracks, to be questioned with flogging, as was the Roman practice, but he desisted on finding out that Paul was a Roman citizen (21:15—22:29).

The next day the Tribune arranged for Paul to be brought before the Jewish Council. Paul caused a violent dissension in the Council when he claimed to be a Pharisee, so the Tribune had him taken to the barracks, where the Lord told him in a vision that he was to bear witness to the Lord in Rome (22:30—23:11).

His Jewish opponents formed a plot to kill Paul in an ambush. When the Tribune heard about the plot from a young relative of Paul, he ordered Paul to be taken, at night and with an impressive guard, to Caesarea, where Felix, the governor of the province, lived. Felix is known to have been procurator between 52 and 60 CE. The Tribune also wrote a letter to Felix informing him of what had happened, mentioning that Paul had not been charged by the Jews with anything deserving death or imprisonment. Felix ordered Paul to be kept in Herod's headquarters until his accusers might arrive (23:12–35).

When they came five days later, together with an advocate named Tertullus, Felix summoned Paul. Tertullus, after the obligatory flattery of the bench, accused Paul of being an agitator and a ringleader of the Nazarene sect. Paul replied, denying the accusations, but admitting to be a follower of 'the Way', a reference that Felix well understood. Felix adjourned the hearing, with Paul to be kept under loose security until a Tribune named Lycius might arrive. Later he had many conversations with Paul, but was obviously hoping for a bribe. Two years later Festus arrived to replace Felix, who left Paul in prison (24:1-27).

Festus was procurator from 60 to 62 CE. The Jews tried to persuade him to take Paul up to Jerusalem, planning an ambush again. Festus declined, but placed Paul on trial again in Caesarea. Again his accusers were unable to prove their charges. Festus offered Paul a trial before himself in Jerusalem, but Paul, a Roman citizen, appealed to the Emperor.

Just as Pilate had sent Jesus to Herod (Luke 23:6-12), Festus arranged for Paul to be brought before King Agrippa. Paul repeated his defence, and told again about his conversion on the way to Damascus. While leaving, Agrippa remarked to Festus that Paul could have been set free had he not appealed to Caesar (25:1—26:32).

Paul's final journey to Rome

Paul and some other prisoners were put on a ship bound for ports along the coast. Again the unnamed companion takes up the story. They were transferred to another ship bound for Rome. The weather was adverse, and the ship was wrecked on Malta. There Paul was bitten by a snake, but suffered no harm. He cured many people. Telling of Paul's solicitude for his fellow passengers, and of his miracles, Luke is demonstrating that Paul continued to be on his mission (27:1—28:10).

When spring arrived they took ship and arrived at Puteoli, near Naples. After a short stay with believers there they arrived in Rome, to be welcomed by more believers. In Rome Paul was allowed to live by himself, under the guard of only one soldier. Once more he reached out to the Jews in Rome, converting some of them. Others, however, refuse to believe, leading Paul to proclaim his mission to the gentiles, who would be prepared to listen.

Luke's story ends with Paul living in Rome and preaching the good news without hindrance. We do not read anything about the persecution that followed or about Paul's death, the circumstances of which are left to tradition (28:11-30).

Chapter 25
Jude and 2 Peter

After Luke's gospel and Acts, which together make up about a quarter of the New Testament, it is time for respite. Jude and 2 Peter are quite short. That is the main reason for taking them out of strict order. Both are quite late, and many think 2 Peter is the last book of the New Testament to be written. Timing is no longer significant, however, and the works remaining to be read, the Book of Revelation and the Johannine literature, were also written towards the end of the first century or at the beginning of the second.

The letter of Jude

There is very little evidence about who wrote this letter, when, or to whom. It purports to be written by Jude, a brother of James, the leader of the church in Jerusalem. It was not written by 'Judas son of James', the apostle referred to in Luke 6:16. In Mark's gospel Jesus is identified by the sceptical Nazarenes as 'the son of Mary and brother of James and Joses and Judas and Simon' (Mk 6:3). Matthew repeats the reference (Mat 13:55). A plausible hypothesis is that, in accordance with the convention in the early Church, the author intended to give authority to his work by identifying himself, in effect, as a brother of Jesus.

The reference to James indicates that Palestine may well have been the most likely place of authorship. It is just as conjectural to decide who were the intended recipients, though the letter seems to assume familiarity with a wide range of Jewish tradition. The readers are addressed as 'those who are called', that is, already Christians, and possibly Palestinian.

When was Jude written?

Various scholars have argued for dates ranging from 50 CE to 120 CE. Brown suggests that the letter could possibly have been written in about 90 CE to 100 CE.

Structure of the letter

After the salutation (vv. 1, 2), the author warns his readers about certain people who are disturbing them. He does not clearly identify what particular doctrine these people have been preaching. He seems to assume that his readers will know to what erroneous teachings they are being exposed, but he refers to perverting grace into licentiousness and denying Christ (v. 4), and indulging in sexual immorality and unnatural lust (vv 7,16). There was some evidence of a heresy by which people claimed that having received the Spirit they were irrevocably saved, and it did not matter what they then did. He then refers to three occasions from Jewish tradition on which God has punished those who disobeyed him (vv 5–8).

In the commentary that follows, Jude continues his polemic against 'these dreamers' (vv 8–19). The reference to the Archangel Michael rebuking Satan probably refers to a lost apocalyptic work called Assumption of Moses, dealing with the death and assumption of Moses into heaven after a struggle for his body between Michael and Satan. The actual terms of the rebuke echo the apocalyptic vision of Zechariah about the attempted interference by Satan in the investiture of Joshua (Zc 3:2).

He then compares the fate of the heretics to that of three biblical sinners. Cain denied God's just judgement (Gen 4:13). Balaam, a prophet, perverted his office for money (Num 31:16). Korah rebelled against Moses and perished (Num 16:1–35). He quotes from Enoch, a collection of apocryphal works of various languages and dates, not all of which are extant. The prophecy attributed to the apostles is not reported anywhere in the New Testament, but is consonant with 1 Timothy 4:1–2.

By contrast with the 'worldly people', he exhorts his readers to build themselves up in faith, tells them how to do so, and urges mercy for those who are wavering (vv 20–23).

The letter concludes with a doxology, praising the God who can save his readers through Jesus Christ (vv 24–25).

2 Peter

Scholars are agreed that this epistle was not written by the person we know as St Peter, despite 1:1. It was written under a pseudonym by someone in the Petrine tradition. It is also clear that the author relied on a well-developed tradition, as he quotes widely from Jude, verbatim from Matthew, and refers to a body of work written by Paul which are known to his readers as part of Scripture (3:16). Brown concludes that the evidence points towards a date in the first half of the second century, about 130 CE, give or take a decade. It is therefore acknowledged that among the works later accepted into the canon, it was the last to be written. It is here dealt with out of strict order because it is so short, has a close connection with Jude, and it seems more appropriate to finish this whole project with the Gospel of John.

Since the letter purports to be a final word from Peter (1:13–15), it is plausible to suggest that it was written in Rome, where Peter had died, and the other scriptures referred to would have been known. It is not addressed to any particular community. The reference to Paul's writings may indicate that it was intended for churches in Rome and Asia Minor. The polemic, especially in chapter 2, does not identify any particular heresy being attacked, except for the errors based on the fact that the second coming had not yet happened (3:1–13).

Structure of the letter

Its division into parts is relatively simple. There is a short opening formula (1:1–2). The body of the epistle can be seen as being in three parts (1:3—3:17). There is a short concluding doxology (3:18).

First (1:3–21), its readers are encouraged to 'become participants of the divine nature' (1:4). The exhortation in vv. 5–7 is remarkable for the variety of virtues extolled. Verse 17 recalls the Transfiguration as described in Matthew 17:5.

Next (2:1–22), false teachers are attacked. In this part there are quite a number of similarities to Jude. The reference to Balaam and his ass is more extensive than in Jude, and is taken from Numbers 22:22–35.

The letter then warns that scoffers will mock them because the Lord has not come again, despite his promise. The author reminds his readers that the second coming had been foretold by the prophets and through the apostles, one of whom he purports to be. God is not bound by time, and the day of the Lord would come like a thief. In the meantime they should lead lives of godliness and holiness, as Paul had also taught (3:1–16).

The letter concludes with an exhortation not to be influenced by the deceit of the lawless ones, but to grow in grace and the knowledge of Jesus, and a doxology giving glory to him now and for ever (3:17–18).

Chapter 26
The Book of Revelation

This book is also known as the Apocalypse. Literally the two words mean the same thing, namely 'unveiling', revelation being from a Latin root and apocalypse from the Greek. It is quite different from the rest of the New Testament and can be difficult for modern people to follow.

Apocalyptic writing is a literary genre the nature of which was fluid and imprecise. It usually consisted of a narrative in which the writer receives knowledge about secrets of the universe or of the future.

It emerged as a new genre of literature in early Jewish tradition commencing sometime in the third century BCE. There were also influences from first the Persian culture and then the Greek, in the period from the fifth to the third centuries BCE. Apocalyptic thinking was extremely influential in Jewish tradition between the second century BCE and third century CE. It was a type of literature well known in the first century and not only to Jews.

Perhaps the most common characteristic of apocalyptic works is that the author receives, often through the intervention of an angel, a vision of another world, replete with vivid imagery and cryptic symbolism, intended to lead the reader to interpret present-day tribulations, such as in times of persecution, in the light of the supernatural and of ultimate salvation. It is not intended to predict particular disasters or to give a physical description of how the world will end.

Apocalypse or prophecy?

It is also difficult to define with any precision the difference between apocalyptic and prophecy. Indeed, the author of the Book of Revelation refers to it as a work of prophecy (1:3, 22:18, 19).

Prophecy, on the other hand, is more strictly spoken of as predicting some future event, often in order to shake listeners out of complacency, though it can also be used to disclose secret knowledge known to God and disclosed for the benefit of others.

Apocalyptic literature is written in symbolism, poetry, and imageries, as well as in a prophecy style familiar in the Hebrew Scriptures. Many parts of the Book of Daniel (ca. 165 BCE) are apocalyptic and there are indications that the author of the Book of Revelation was influenced by the Book of Daniel. We can also see gleanings of this style in Matthew 24–25; Mark 13; Luke 21; Revelation 1:2–4; 19:9; 22:7–19.

Author and Place

The author names himself as John. Although there was an early tradition identifying him as an apostle, it is now clear that he was neither John the son of Zebedee nor the author of the Gospel or the letters of John. The Greek style is the poorest in the New Testament, and there are indications that the author's native language was Hebrew or Aramaic. He knew and was known to the Christians in the seven churches of Asia Minor to whom the work is addressed.

He also wrote that the vision came to him while he was on the island of Patmos, a Greek island in the Aegean Sea about 25 km west of Ephesus (1:9). A local tradition is that he had been banished in exile to the island during a persecution in the reign of Domitian (81 CE—96 CE). Another suggestion is that he was in solitude on the island in order to hear 'the word of God and the testimony of Jesus.'

Date

The book is the last appearing in our Bibles, but that does not mean that it was the last to be written. That distinction probably belongs to 2 Peter, which may well have been written early in the second century.

If the hypothesis is accepted that John was banished to Patmos during the reign of Domitian, which is not inconsistent with known facts, it would indicate a date of about 92 CE to 96 CE . This has the support of such authorities as Irenaeus, Eusebius and St Jerome. There is little support for alternative theories that the book was written earlier, during the reigns of Nero or Claudius.

Division

The book is, by its very nature, cryptic and complex, and, especially on this occasion, when it is being read as a whole for the first time, the best approach is simply to take up the book and read it. It should first be read as it would have been by the people to whom it was addressed, namely Christians towards the end of the first century, after the Temple in Jerusalem had been destroyed and there had been a number of persecutions by Roman emperors. They were being exhorted to be patient, as in the end God would triumph over all evil and suffering.

In his recent book, *Reading the New Testament in the Church* (see further reading, page 209), Moloney suggests that we may instead read the book as 'affirming that God's victory over evil has already been won in the death and resurrection of Jesus, and that victory has always been present' (182).

Although it has been said that, of all the New Testament works, this is the one that most calls out for commentary, it is beyond the scope of this present work to attempt any detailed analysis.

The following division, adapted from Brown, may help the reader not to get lost.

1 Prologue (1:1–3)

2 Epistles to the seven churches

Salutation (1:4–8).
Vision of Christ as the Son of Man (1:9–20)
Epistles to the seven churches (2:1–3:22).

Fig. 26.1

The seven cities are situated in the western part of Asia Minor, or modern Turkey. They are listed in an order that suggests a semicircular, or horseshoe shaped path in a clockwise direction, beginning with Ephesus, the most famous, on the coast, going north through Smyrna to Pergamum, then south-east and south through Thyatira, Sardis, Philadelphia and Laodicea, which is roughly inland and east from Ephesus.

Three sorts of problems confront the churches: false teaching, persecution and complacency. The letters demonstrate that, by the time Revelation was written, in some places there was no longer the initial zeal that had characterised the early church, as described in the first part of Acts.

- Ephesus is praised for its works and endurance, but chided for having abandoned the love that it had at first (2:1–7).
- Smyrna is faced with persecution and encouraged to persevere (2:8–11).
- In Pergamum a temple to the godhead of Caesar had been built in 29 BCE. The church was holding fast, though there were some who held pagan beliefs. Nothing is known about the Nicolaitans (2:12–17).

- The love, faith and endurance of the church in Thyatira are praised, but they are warned against a claimed prophetess, Jezebel (2:18–29).
- Sardis has the name of being a vibrant church, but is in fact dead, except for a few worthy ones (3:1–6).
- Those in Philadelphia are praised for having kept the faith though having little power (3:7–13).
- Laodicea is reproved for being neither hot nor cold, but lukewarm (3:14–22).

3 Part 1 of revelatory experience

Vision of God enthroned (4:1–11)
The lamb able to open the sealed scrolls (5:1–14
Seven seals and the servants of God (6:1–8:1)
Seven angels with trumpets (8:2–11:19).

4 Part 2 of revelatory experience

Vision of the dragon and the beasts (12:1—13:18
The lamb, angels and the Son of Man (14:1–20)
Seven plagues (15:1–8)
Seven bowls of the wrath of God (16:1–21
Fall of Babylon, the great harlot (17:1—19:10)
Fall of Satan (19:11—20:3).
The end of times, victory of Christ and the New Jerusalem (20:4—22:7).

5 Epilogue and blessing (22:8–21).

- *Though the church is still persecuted in some countries, we in Australia need to be on our guard more against false teaching and especially complacency.*
- *Probably no other piece of literature has inspired more art, music and literature than the Book of Revelation—why do you think this is?*

Chapter 27
Johannine literature

The Gospel and the Letters

The Gospel and the letters that bear the name of John are dealt with together under the rubric of Joannine Literature. This is not because they were certainly all written by the same person. Probably they were not. They were, however, addressed to members of the same community, and the letters were practically contemporaneous with and arose out of reactions within that community to certain aspects of the Gospel.

Authorship and dates

Among the disciples referred to in John's Gospel, one is chosen for special mention. At the Last Supper it was he who asked Jesus who it was that was to betray him. He is called 'the one whom Jesus loved' (13:21–26). He was known to the high priest, and enabled Peter to gain access to the courtyard after Jesus' arrest (18:15–16). He stood with Mary at the foot of the cross when Jesus committed her to his care (19:25–27). He ran with Peter to the tomb when Mary Magdalen told them that the Lord was no longer there (20:2–10). He is not identified by name, and is not named as an apostle (John does not use that word), nor even as one of the twelve. He is referred to conventionally as 'the Beloved Disciple'.

Until the 18th century it was assumed that the Beloved Disciple was John the apostle, the son of Zebedee, and that it was he who personally wrote the Gospel and each of the letters. During the last two centuries this assumption has been the subject of a great deal of scholarly debate.

A recent and credible hypothesis, though not yet universally accepted, is that there were three stages in the writing of the Gospel.[1] That there was more than one is clear. The natural sequence from 14:31 to 18:1 shows that chapters 15–17 were additions. There are two endings, chapter 21 being added after the natural ending of 20:30.

According to this theory, the first edition, written early in the second half of the first century, was a narrative of the life, death and resurrection of Jesus, and included all the miracles of the present gospel. The community to which it was addressed largely consisted of Jewish Christians. Their increasing understanding of what the Jesus event meant led to conflict with 'the Jews'. This phrase in John must always be understood as referring, not to the Jewish people, but to the authorities and those who regarded the beliefs of the Christian Jews as blasphemy. Despite their desire to continue to be included within Judaism, the Christians were finally excluded from the synagogues.

A different author added to the first edition material that emphasised the reception of the Spirit through belief in Jesus, and the difficulties caused by the exclusion from the synagogues.

Exclusion from the synagogues, such a noticeable theme in the Gospel, might be described as an external crisis. Some time later, the community was experiencing another crisis, an internal division, about correct belief and correct conduct. In response, a disciple who had been an eyewitness of the ministry of Jesus, by now old enough to be called 'the Elder', wrote the three letters in order to clarify the tradition of which he had been a founding witness.

When the letters were written is uncertain. Exclusion from the synagogues was no longer a topic to be dealt with. The point of the letters is concern about people preaching wrong doctrine. It is difficult to identify with any precision from the discursive content of the letters just what were the false doctrines of those whom we may here call the opponents.

There were some at the time who held that having received the Spirit they were so identified with God as to be unable to sin. Obviously such a heresy could lead to a carefree indulgence in disgraceful behaviour.

---

1. Urban C. von Wahlde, *The Gospel and Letters of John*, Grand Rapids Mich., Eerdmans 2010.

There were also the Gnostics, who taught that salvation was achieved through a particular type of knowledge (*gnosis* being Greek for knowledge). Many of them drew a distinction between Jesus, who was man, and Christ, a semidivine being who took possession of Jesus until his crucifixion. John insists that Jesus was both truly human and truly God.

The Elder then died, perhaps between 80 and 90 CE, though all dates about the Joannine literature are speculative.

Soon after the death of the Elder, a third author composed the final edition of the Gospel, which confirmed the views of the Elder (whom the community by now referred to as 'the beloved disciple'), explained his death and addressed new issues that had arisen. This edition was written probably towards the end of the first century or the beginning of the second, and may well have been addressed to a community in and around Ephesus.

Chapter 28
The letters of John

1 John

This epistle comprises four simple elements:
a prologue (1:1-4)
God as light (1:5-3:10)
God as love (3:11—5:12) and
an epilogue (5:13-21).

A notable characteristic is the series of antitheses, which reflect those in the Gospel, namely, light and darkness, sin and forgiveness, obedience and disobedience, love and being in the light, hatred and being in darkness. The work should not be analysed logically, as the argument is built up by the repetition in different forms of a small number of basic ideas.

The prologue founds what is to follow on the personal experience of the writer, who had been a witness of the ministry of Jesus (1:1-4).

The first section of the body of the letter emphasises 'that God is light and in him there is no darkness at all' (1:5-7). Immediately John attacks those who do not acknowledge that their wrongdoing is sin, and who claim to know God while not keeping his commandments, especially the commandment to love one's neighbour (1:8—2:11). Those who are then addressed as fathers are probably those who have been Christian for some time, while the children and young ones may be recent converts. They are warned against love of the world and its desires (2:12-17).

The false teachers who had separated from the community are antichrists, while those who hold to the truth abide in the Father and the Son, and are God's children. They may be confident that they will not be ashamed when Christ comes again (2:18—3:3). John repeats his message that those who abide in God do not sin, while those who do sin do not abide in God (3:4-10).

The second section concentrates on obeying Jesus' commandment to love, by which we abide in him (3:11-24). John provides a test for discerning false prophets. Those who acknowledge that Jesus came from God in the flesh, and who listen to the author, know God, who is love. Those who love God must respond by loving their brothers and sisters also (4:1-21). Faith in Jesus as the son of God, shown by our obedience to his commandment of love, enables us to conquer the world (5:1-5).

The next passage (5:6-8), is obscure. Centuries after the epistle was written, verses were inserted, reflecting later concepts of the Trinity. Scholars refer to the added material as 'the Johannine comma' (comma meaning a short clause).

> The Johannine comma
> 'Because there are three who testify *in heaven*: *Father Word and Holy Spirit and these three are one*; and there are three who testify *on earth*: the Spirit and the water and the blood; and the three are of one accord.'

It is God who has testified that we have eternal life through his son (5:9-12).

The epilogue states John's purpose in writing the letter, 'so that you may know that you have eternal life' (5: 13). Jesus answers our prayers, and will forgive those whose sin is not mortal. This distinction, between sin that is mortal and sin that is not, is not the same distinction as in our later moral theology. The deadly sin would appear to be joining the opponents, a form of apostasy (5:14-17).

The letter ends with a proclamation that Jesus is true God and eternal life, and an exhortation to keep from the false ideas about Christ, which are a form of idolatry (5:18-21).

2 John

The writer does not give us his name. He describes himself as 'the Elder'. This description would be consistent with the theory that the Beloved Disciple, a young man at the time of Jesus death, would by now have been of quite an advanced age and highly respected in his community. He is writing to a community that he calls 'the elect lady and her children', a church probably at some distance from his own.

He begins with a prayer in the manner common in Christian letters at the time (1-3). The community to whom he is writing is orthodox in belief and in keeping the commandment of love, but deceivers are on their way to them, against whom they should be on their guard (4-11).

He ends the letter expressing an apology for its brevity, his hope to visit them, and greetings from the church from which he is writing (12-13).

3 John

This is the shortest book in the New Testament. Again, the writer identifies himself as 'the Elder'. However, this time he is writing, not to a community, but to one Gaius, of whom nothing is known to us. He is obviously well known to the Elder, admired by him, and prominent in his own community (1-4). Brothers, possibly itinerant missionaries sent out by the Elder and carrying the letter, are visiting his community and the Elder urges Gaius to be hospitable to them (5-8).

We also know nothing about Diotrephes, except that he is a member of Gaius's church, but he does not accept the authority of the Elder. He even tries to exclude the brothers who are visiting them. Demetrius on the other hand, either another member of the community or a misssionary sent to them by the Elder, has the truth and is commended by the Elder (9-12).

This letter also expresses an apology for its brevity, and a desire to visit the community. It ends with a prayer for peace, and greetings from the Elder's community (13-15).

Chapter 29
The Gospel according to John

Fig. 29.1

When we come to read the Gospel of John as a whole there is no need for us to concern ourselves about details of authorship. The Gospel derives its authority for us, not from having been written by the one apostolic author, but from its consistent and coherent message. It was written to a community already Christian, to challenge believers to think more deeply about who and what Jesus was, and how they should relate to him and to each other.

It differs from the synoptic gospels in many ways, and does not appear to be directly dependent upon them, but in essentials it is based on a tradition common to them all. Matters that are common include the proclamation of John the Baptist that he was the precursor of the Son of God (1:19–29), the purification of the temple (2:13–22), the feeding of the five thousand and walking on the water (6:1–21), the plot to kill Jesus (11:45–54), the triumphal entry into Jerusalem (12:12–19), the trial before Pilate and the crucifixion (18:28—19:30), and the empty tomb (20:1–10).

Elements peculiar to John include Jesus being conscious of having pre-existed with God (3:13, 8:52–58, 17:5, 24), the miracles at Cana, the raising of Lazarus, his public life extending over three years, his death being on the day of preparation before Passover instead of shortly after the feast, and the alternation of his ministry between Galilee and Judaea, with the major focus being on confrontations in Judaea.

There are fewer miracles in John, but he provides much more detail in each. There are long discourses and dialogues, often featuring 'I am' statements. There is no casting out of demons nor any concentration on the Kingdom of God.

There are some notable characteristics of style. One is the frequent use of misunderstanding. Jesus may use a metaphor to present his message. The person hearing it treats it literally, allowing Jesus or John an opportunity to explain or expand his message, as when Jesus spoke of destroying the Temple and raising it up after three days (2:19–22).

In much the same vein, John often uses words that have more than one meaning, indicating several layers of meaning in the one utterance, as in the phrase 'the Lamb of God' (1: 29–36), meaning an apocalyptic lamb, the Paschal lamb, and the servant who went willingly to slaughter like a lamb in Isaiah 53:7. Sometimes the listener will take one meaning while Jesus intends the other, as when he discusses being 'born again' with Nicodemus (3:6-10).

There is also irony. A character may make a derogatory or incredulous comment about Jesus, false in the sense that they intend, but true in a way that the speaker does not realise, as when the Samaritan woman asks Jesus whether he is greater than Jacob (4:11-14).

John has articulated the themes that he wishes to emphasise about Jesus by the careful structure that he has imposed upon the gospel.

The Prologue (1:1–18)

A theological introduction to the career of Jesus as the incarnate Word who became man.

Part 1: The Book of Signs (1:19—12:50)

A   *Beginning of revelation of Jesus*

John the Baptist and disciples (1:19-51)
First Cana miracle (2:1-12)
Cleansing the Temple (2:13-25)
Nicodemus (3:1-21)
John the Baptist (3:22-36)
Samaritans (4:1-42)
Second Cana miracle (4:43-54)

B   *Hebrew feasts*

Sabbath (5:1-47)
Passover (6:1-71)
Tabernacles (7:1-10:21)
Dedication (10:22-42)

C   *Jesus turns towards the hour*

Raising of Lazarus (11:1-44)
Plot to kill Jesus (11:45-57)
Jesus is anointed (12:1-8)
Entry into Jerusalem (12:9-19)

The hour has come (12:20-36)
Unbelief of the people (12:37-43)
Jesus summarises his message (12:44-50)

Part 2: The Book of Glory (13:1—20:31)

A   *The Last Supper*

Washing of the feet (13:1-20)
Betrayal by Judas (13:21-30)
New commandment of love (13:31-35)
Peter's denial foretold (13:36-38)
Jesus the way to the father (Ch 14)
The true vine (Ch 15)
Departure to the father and promise to send the spirit (Ch 16)
Prayer for all disciples (Ch 17)

B   *Passion and death*

Betrayal and arrest (18:1-12)
Trial before high priest and Peter's denial (18:13-27)
Trial before Pilate (18:28- 19:16)
Crucifixion and death (19:17-37)
Burial (19:38-42)

C   *Resurrection*

The empty tomb (20:1-10)
Appearance to Mary Magdalene (20:11-18)
Appearance to disciples (20:19-29)
Purpose in writing (20:30-31)

Epilogue (Chapter 21)

Appearance in Galilee (21:1-23)
Second conclusion (21:24-25)

The prologue (1:1–18)

Unlike those of Matthew and Luke, John's Gospel does not begin with an infancy story, but 'in the beginning', with God. The story of creation in Genesis begins with exactly the same words. God became part of his creation, as 'the Word', bringing light. As with all words, the Word is meant to be heard by others.

This gospel does not end with an ascension into heaven. It begins with Jesus' coming down from heaven (1:14).

As we read the prologue, we are told that Jesus is God and that those who accept his enlightenment become children of God. The characters in the story that is to follow have not been told. What follows describes how some came to believe, while others did not.

Part 1: The Book of Signs (1:19—12:50)

Days of preparation (1:19-51)

The story begins with increasing recognition over a series of days of who Jesus is. John bestows on Jesus at the beginning of his gospel the titles that appear scattered and later in the other gospels.

By contrast with the other evangelists, in this story John does not baptise Jesus, but proclaims that he is only the precursor of the one who is the Lamb of God and the Son of God. Andrew and another disciple leave John to follow Jesus. Andrew tells his brother Simon that he has found the Messiah and Jesus renames Simon as Peter, the rock.

Jesus then finds Philip, who persuades Nathaniel to meet Jesus, telling him that he has found the one foretold by Moses and the prophets. Impressed by the knowledge that Jesus has of his prior whereabouts, Nathaniel proclaims Jesus as Son of God and King of Israel. The disciples believe in Jesus, but their faith is not yet soundly based. What kind of faith is called for?

From Cana to Cana (Chapters 2—4)

Between the first and second of the signs that Jesus did to reveal his glory, the gospel recounts a series of contrasting stories that begin to answer this question.

At the first, the wedding feast at Cana, Mary his mother demonstrates her complete trust in his efficacy. Just 'Do whatever he tells you' is all she need say (2:1-12).

As the Passover approached, Jesus went up to the Temple in Jerusalem, and drove out the traders and money changers. 'The Jews' asked him for a sign. He foretold his resurrection. 'The Jews' did not believe him (2:13-21). His disciples, after his resurrection, remembered his words and believed (2:22). Other Jews, not part of the establishment, who were in Jerusalem at the time, believed because of the signs that Jesus did, an incomplete faith (2:23).

> It is necessary to distinguish the Jewish officials and others who were opposed to Jesus from the general body of the Jewish people, many of whom became disciples or were indifferent to him. Quotation marks are used here to indicate the former.

The next story is ambivalent. Nicodemus, a member of the Sanhedrin, came to visit Jesus. He came by night. Was this because he was afraid of those opposed to Jesus, or was it because he came still in the darkness of ignorance? We shall read two more episodes about Nicodemus in this gospel, and then ponder whether, at the end, he has come to true faith in Jesus. On this first visit he initially appears well intentioned and open-minded. However, when Jesus tells him that he must be 'born from above', he misunderstands what Jesus is talking about. He can think only of becoming a Jew, and thus one of God's chosen people, by being born of a Jewish mother. Despite being a learned man and a 'teacher of Israel' he seems to persist in his misunderstanding. Ironically, to Nicodemus, who began the conversation by saying, 'We know that you are a teacher who comes from God,' but who obviously does not know how true that is, Jesus ironically responds, 'We speak of what we know' and tells him that he, Jesus, has descended from heaven and that faith in him is necessary in order to have eternal life. John does not tell us explicitly what Nicodemus's reaction is (3:1-21).

By contrast, John the Baptist demonstrates his true faith, declaring that he was merely sent ahead of the Messiah, who was the one truly sent from heaven and belief in whom gives eternal life (3:22-36).

On his way through Samaria back to Galilee Jesus encountered a Samaritan woman by the well of Jacob. At first she, like Nicodemus, was unable to see past the literal meaning of the words he used when speaking to her about living water. She starts from a state of no faith. Impressed, however, by his knowledge of her marital status she acknowledged that he was a prophet. When he claimed to her that he was the Messiah, she returned to her village to tell her people what he had been able to tell her, and wondered to them whether perhaps he could indeed be the Messiah. She had started on the way to true faith. Many of the Samaritans, however, believed in Jesus, not only because of what she had told them, but because of what he said to them over the next two days. They said, 'We know that this is truly the Saviour of the world.' They had arrived at true faith (4:1-42).

Jesus then returned again to Cana in Galilee where he had given his first sign. This was to be where he would give his second. A royal official asked him to heal his son, who lay ill in Capernaum. Jesus challenged him, asserting that his faith depended upon a miracle. The official simply responded, 'Sir come down before my little boy dies'. He had arrived at true faith, as Jesus acknowledged. When he arrived back at his home to find his son healed, his whole household joined him in belief (4:46-54).

In this group of episodes between the two signs at Cana, John has depicted the refusal to believe of 'the Jews', the journey to faith of Mary, John the Baptist, other Jews in Jerusalem, and perhaps Nicodemus, all from the world of Judaism. Then he tells of the journeys on the same road of the Samaritan woman, the Samaritan villagers, and the Royal official, all from outside Judaism. Faith in Jesus is possible for all humankind (4:43-54).

- *Where are we on that road?*

Jewish Feasts (Chapters 5—10)

The Johannine community had been cast out of the synagogues, and separated from their traditional roots. They wondered what was their relationship now with the God of Israel. Over the next six chapters Jesus is depicted as replacing or restating some significant aspect of four of the most important festivals of the Jewish religion. At the same time, we read of the increasing hostility of 'the Jews' towards Jesus.

The Sabbath—*Shabbat*

The first is the Sabbath, the seventh day of the Jewish week and is the day of rest and abstention from work as commanded by God (Ex 20:11; Deut 5:12-15).

Jesus healed a lame man and also ordered him to take up his bedding and walk. Both the healing and the walking while carrying the mat would have been seen as violating the Sabbath. 'The Jews' began their persecution. Jesus responded by claiming that he and his Father were both still working. 'The Jews' correctly perceived that Jesus was not only breaking the Sabbath, but also making himself equal to God. They sought all the more to kill him. Jesus did not resile from their conclusion, but reinforced his claim to be doing what the Father was doing. Not only had John the Baptist testified to the truth about Jesus, but the Father himself had done so by the works that he was doing, as had also the Scriptures and Moses (5:1-47).

Passover—*Pesach*

At Passover the Jewish people celebrate the memory of their deliverance from slavery in Egypt under the leadership of Moses, during which they had passed through the Red Sea, and had been provided with 'manna from heaven' when they were hungry in the desert.

As the feast of the Passover approached, Jesus crossed the Sea of Galilee, and multiplied the loaves and fishes to feed the large crowd of people who had followed him there. The people misunderstood this sign, thinking that he was the prophet who would deliver them from the Romans, and wanting to make him king.

He withdrew to the mountain, and later came to his disciples, walking on the water of the Sea of Galilee. The crowd followed him to Capernaum, where Jesus instructed them that he was the bread of life, and that all who believed in him would have eternal life, unlike their ancestors who had eaten manna in the desert but had afterwards died.

When he then said that the bread that he would give for the life of the world was his flesh, 'the Jews' asked, 'How can this man give us his flesh to eat?' Jesus repeated his teaching, and many of his disciples left him. Peter spoke for the twelve, proclaiming that they would not leave, that he was the Holy One of God and had the words of eternal life. Jesus revealed his knowledge that Judas, although one of the twelve, would betray him (6:1-71).

Festival of Booths—*Sukkot*

Also called Tabernacles, this feast centred on the Temple in Jerusalem. Many made a pilgrimage there, to take part in ceremonies lasting over seven days. Participants were expected to provide a booth in which to sleep and eat during the feast. Each morning the priests would bring up a container of water from the pool of Siloam to the temple for use in the temple, linking the festival with the gift of rain. At night huge torches were ceremonially lit in the temple symbolising that the temple was the light of all Jerusalem. Each day at dawn the priests went to face East at the east gate of the temple, and at dawn turned to face West, recalling the apostasy of earlier generations and turning away from them to look to the Holy of Holies and profess faith in the one true God.

As the festival approached, Jesus at first declined to leave Galilee, knowing that 'the Jews' in Judaea wanted to kill him. He later went up to Jerusalem in secret. There is a constant theme of conflict in this chapter. First there was disagreement with his family about going up to the feast (7:1-9). Next, as he preached in the temple, there was conflict among his listeners. At issue was his claim to be the Messiah (7:10-31). On the last day, the most important of the festival, he proclaimed that he would satisfy the thirst of any who believed in him. By his death and the gift of the spirit he would replace the ritual water of the feast. There was renewed conflict about whether he was the Messiah (7:37-44).

The Pharisees and chief priests sent the temple police to arrest him. They demonstrated their disbelief when the police reported to them (7:32-36, 45-49). When the fair-minded Nicodemus protested that they were acting against the law by condemning Jesus unheard, they rounded on him also. He appeared at this stage to be more interested in the legality of their actions, rather than belief in Jesus (7:50-52).

The next passage, about the woman taken in adultery, appears to be out of context, and is enclosed in brackets in NRSV, indicating that possibly it was a later addition. It is, however, a beautiful indication of Jesus' mercy toward sinners. He makes it clear that he is not one of those who would condemn her to death, but exhorts her to turn away from sin (8:1-11).

The gospel then returns to the theme of the feast. Jesus announces that he is the light of the world. Thus he replaces the lights lit in the temple. He answers the objection that he is merely testifying on his own behalf by claiming that the father who sent him also testifies to him (8:12-30). That led to a long dispute about descent from Abraham, at the end of which Jesus said, 'I tell you, before Abraham was, I am'. This was so explicit a claim to be God that they immediately took up stones to kill him (8:31-59).

John then most skilfully combines the themes of light, water and faith in the story of the man born blind. On the Sabbath, saying again that he was the light of the world, Jesus sent the blind man to wash in the pool of Siloam. He immediately obeyed, and became able to see for the first time. Questioned by the Pharisees he proclaimed that Jesus was a prophet. His parents told them that their son should answer for himself, because they were afraid of being put out of the synagogue. He then replied to their accusations that if Jesus were not from God he could do nothing, let alone give sight to a man born blind. Meeting Jesus, and now seeing him for the first time, he proclaimed his belief and worshipped Jesus. He provides another instance of someone coming to true faith. The Pharisees remained blind (9:1-41).

That led Jesus to tell the parable of the Good Shepherd, who will lay down his life for his sheep. He expressly stated that no one would take his life from him, but that he would lay it down of his own accord, obeying his father's command. Dissent among the Jews continued (10:1-21).

Festival of Dedication—*Chanukkah*

The Feast of Dedication commemorated the reconstruction of the Temple and the dedication of the altar by Judas Maccabeus in 164 BCE, after decades of desecration by Syrian rulers. The Temple became again the place where God dwelt amongst his people.

At this festival 'the Jews' challenged Jesus to tell plainly whether he was the Messiah. He answered bluntly that he had already done so, but they would not believe. When he said 'the Father and I are one' they took up stones with which to kill him for blasphemy. He was revealing that he was the visible presence of God among them, replacing the need for a temple. 'The Jews' again tried to arrest him, but he escaped and returned across the Jordan to where John had been baptising at the beginning of his mission (1: 29). There many more came to believe in him (10:22-42).

Jesus turns towards the hour (Chapters 11—12)

These chapters form a bridge between the Book of Signs and the Book of Glory. Martha and Mary sent a message from Bethany asking Jesus to come to them, because their brother Lazarus was ill. After an initial delay he announced his intention to return to Judaea, despite the protests of his disciples. He told them that Lazarus was dead, but that he was going to him for their sake, so that they might believe. Twice in this story John has Jesus state that God's glory and his own are to be demonstrated by the miracle (11:4, 40).

Jesus is about to raise Lazarus from the dead, but Lazarus will die again. This is a resuscitation, not resurrection to eternal life. Jesus, however, is both the resurrection and the life, and belief in him leads to eternal life. Martha believes (11:17-27).

When the council heard about the miracle, they decided formally to put Jesus to death. The high priest prophesied that his death would be, not only for Israel, but to gather into one the dispersed children of God (11:46-53).

Mary anointed Jesus, unwittingly in preparation for his death and burial. As crowds gathered to see Lazarus, the chief priests decided to put him to death as well as Jesus.

Jesus told some Greeks who had come to the Passover festival that the hour had come for him to be glorified. He prayed to the father, 'Father, glorify your name.' A voice from heaven replied, 'I have glorified it, and will glorify it again'. Jesus foretold his crucifixion, saying that when he was lifted up from the earth, he would draw all people to himself.

Despite all the signs he had performed in their presence, 'the Jews' did not believe in him, and many of those who did believe would not confess it, for fear of being put out of the synagogues, 'for they loved human glory more than the glory that comes from God.' John is here using the Greek word *doxa* (translated 'glory'), to mean both the esteem of others as well as the living presence of God in their midst in Jesus (12:1–43).

> *Doxa* (from the ancient Greek 'to expect', 'to seem') is a Greek word meaning common belief or popular opinion. The word *doxa* picked up a new meaning between the 3rd and 1st centuries BCE when the Septuagint translated the Hebrew word for 'glory' as *doxa*. Hence the word 'doxology'—an expression of praise to the Holy Trinity, the Father, the Son and the Holy Spirit.

Jesus summarised his teaching. Belief in him is belief in the one who sent him. He had come, not to judge the world, but to save it. He is the light who has come into the world, and judgement consists of the difference between those who believe in him and those who reject him (12:44–50).

Part 2: The Book of Glory (13:1—20:31)

The last supper (Chapters 13—17)

Before the festival of Passover Jesus had supper with his disciples, knowing that his hour had come. These chapters contain his last discourse, much longer and more detailed than in the other gospels.

In an action designed to demonstrate to his disciples the necessity for service of each other, Jesus washed their feet, though he was their Lord and Teacher.

He declared that one of them would betray him. John here introduces 'the disciple whom Jesus loved'. At Peter's behest he asked Jesus who the traitor could be. Jesus indicated discreetly that it was Judas, who went out into the darkness of the night.

Again Jesus spoke of glorification, and gave them his new commandment, that they should love one another as he loved them. This love is to be the mark of the true disciple. Peter brashly claimed that he would lay down his life for Jesus, but Jesus foretold that he would deny him three times before the cock crowed in the morning (13:1–38).

Jesus began to console his disciples by explaining that, although he was about to go to the Father, he would prepare a place for them. He told Thomas that he was the way, truth and the life, and explained to Philip that to see him was to see the Father.

Until this point in the story, Jesus has been the unique revelation of the Father. Here he introduces another, the Advocate, the Spirit of truth, who would teach them everything and remind them of all that Jesus had said (14:1–31). The chapter finishes with Jesus saying, 'Rise, let us be on our way'.

Chapter 18 begins, 'After he had said these words he went out with his disciples'.

Chapters 15, 16 and 17 are additions to the original gospel. However, they contain such beautiful expositions by Jesus of his message that they do not interrupt John's portrait of him. They enhance it.

Jesus expounds his metaphor of himself as the true vine, his Father the vine grower, and his followers the branches. We are fruitful only if we abide in him as he does in the Father. His commandment is, again, to love one another as he has loved us (15:1–17). The world would indeed hate his followers, as it has hated him, but in order to strengthen them, he would send the Spirit to testify on his behalf, as they should also do (15:18—16:4).

He tells them that he is about to go to his Father, in order to send the Spirit to them, but again they do not at first understand. He has to spell it out plainly for them. There was to be a time between the present, when he has to leave, and a time in the future when he would be with them. As with a woman giving birth, their sorrow would turn into joy (16:4–33).

Then he made his final prayer to his Father for his disciples. The hour had come for him to be glorified and to glorify his Father. His disciples had believed in him, and he asked the Father to protect them from evil, and not only them, but all who would believe in him through their word (17:1–26).

Passion and Death (Chapters 18, 19)

In the other gospels, Jesus had been praying in agony when Judas arrived with the soldiers to arrest him. In John, when Jesus tells the soldiers that he is the Jesus of Nazareth whom they are seeking, it is the soldiers who fall down. When Peter attacked a servant of the high priest with a sword Jesus told him to put it away. He was ready to die in accordance with his father's will. He allowed himself to be arrested. Throughout the whole of the story of his passion and death Jesus is in control (18:1–12).

His captors bound him, and took him first to Annas, the father-in-law of the high priest. Peter and another disciple, perhaps the one whom Jesus loved, followed them into the courtyard, where Peter made his first denial.

The high priest questioned Jesus, to be told by Jesus that he had preached openly. His time for preaching had finished. Now it would be for his disciples. Annas sent him bound to the high priest. Meanwhile, Peter, warming himself in the courtyard, again denied Jesus twice, and the cock crowed (18:13–27).

Because only the Romans could lawfully crucify a criminal, 'the Jews' took Jesus from Caiaphas to Pilate's headquarters. They remained outside, to avoid ritual defilement. There is then a series of scenes where Pilate speaks to Jesus in his headquarters, and comes out to speak to 'the Jews'.

Pilate asked Jesus whether he was the King of the Jews. On a number of earlier occasions Jesus had found it necessary to avoid being treated as an earthly king by enthusiastic followers. Now he made it explicit to Pilate that his kingdom was not of this world. Pilate cynically made clear that truth was not his primary consideration. His main concern was to avoid disorder. He went out again and told 'the Jews' that he found no case against Jesus. Seeking to mollify the crowd, he offered to release Jesus, whom he called the King of the Jews, for the Passover. The crowd chose Barabbas, a bandit in custody.

Pilate obviously thought that more questioning was called for. The Roman custom was often to administer a flogging in order to induce a prisoner to cooperate in the questioning. Pilate had Jesus flogged, and the soldiers mockingly ridiculed Jesus again as King of the Jews. Their mockery is an ironic declaration of the truth, which is aimed at the Jews, as well as at Jesus.

Pilate again came out to proclaim his belief in Jesus' innocence. Although he says, 'I am bringing him out again', Jesus was not led out. He came out. John uses the same Greek phrase meaning 'he came out' in respect of Jesus as in respect of Pilate at 18:29, 38 and 19:4. He came out still crowned and robed as a king. Whereas before (18:39) Pilate had sarcastically described Jesus to them as 'the King of the Jews', on this occasion he said simply, 'Here is the man!' This may well have been in his mind a less confrontational and more conciliatory description. Pilate was trying to show that this pathetic Jesus was no threat to anyone. It is clear, however, that Jesus did not see himself as pathetic. He was in control of his own destiny, doing the will of his father.

Pilate's suggestion that 'the Jews' should do their own crucifying was obviously not serious, and they continued to press Pilate to effect it. Now at last they came to the real basis of their desire for blood. It was not because Jesus claimed to be a king, or posed a threat to the Romans, but because he made himself the Son of God.

Pilate was now more afraid than ever. It was becoming more and more clear that he would have to make a decision, not merely about the politics of his position, but about truth. Pilate asked Jesus where he was from, meaning 'exactly who are you?' Jesus gave him no answer. Pilate had already shown that he could not or would not understand what Jesus had explained to him about being a king. Jesus has already answered Pilate's question, if only Pilate would listen. John depicts Pilate as on trial, as well as or more than Jesus, and he will be convicted.

When Pilate blustered about his earthly power, Jesus answered him at length. Pilate would not have any power at all unless it had been given to him from above. He was but an unwitting instrument of God's power. Jesus had said that no one could take his life from him, but he had power to lay it down and to take it up again, in accordance with the Father's will.

Pilate's further efforts to release Jesus were met by a threat that really did cause him to fear, namely a complaint to the emperor that he had set free a king. He handed Jesus over to be crucified (18:28—19:16).

John's description of the crucifixion is relatively short, but crammed with significant details. Pilate proclaimed to all mankind that Jesus was king with the plaque written in the languages of the Greeks, the Jews and the Romans. He refused the request of 'the Jews' that he should tone down the irony.

Like his seamless robe, Jesus' kingdom would not be torn apart even at the hands of his enemies. His kingdom would be founded on faith and love, not mere flesh and blood, as he showed by joining together as one Mary, his first believer and the Beloved Disciple.

When he knew that he had finished the task given to him by his Father, he gave up his Spirit and died. There is no Pentecost in John. The gift of the Spirit is bestowed from the cross at the moment of Jesus' death. The flowing of the water from his side symbolises his gift of the Spirit, and the failure to break his legs showed that he was the foretold Lamb of God (19:17-37).

Two Jews who had encountered Jesus went to Pilate to ask for the body of Jesus, to bury it. One was Joseph of Arimathea, who has not previously been mentioned in John's gospel. However, all three synoptic gospels name him as the person who buried Jesus (see Mk 15:43-46; Matt 27:57-60; Luke 23:50-53). He was rich, and a member of the Sanhedrin who had not been a party to their plans. John depicts him as having been a secret disciple, for fear of 'the Jews'. Going to Pilate and asking for the body was surely a sufficiently public act to demonstrate that he had at last come to true faith.

The other was Nicodemus, also a member of the Sanhedrin, who had been favourably disposed towards Jesus, but when last mentioned (7:50-2), had not proclaimed his faith in him. Academic opinions differ about Nicodemus. However, John specifies the amount of spices he brought to the burial. The quantity and value was such as to be fit for the burial of a king. There is no suggestion that the burial took place in secret. In fact, by contrast with his first having come to Jesus by night, the burial takes place on the day of preparation—the day before Shabbat. May we not conclude that at last he also had come to true faith, despite his earlier inability to see the truth about who Jesus was?

Resurrection (Chapter 20)

The Resurrection may be seen as a drama with an introduction and two acts.

As an introduction Mary Magdalen went to the tomb in the dark of early morning, to find that the stone had been removed. She went to tell Peter and the Beloved Disciple (20:1-2).

In the first scene of the first act, Peter and the Beloved Disciple ran to the tomb. The Beloved Disciple arrived first, but, although he looked in and saw the discarded wrappings, he did not go in until Peter arrived. Peter then went into the tomb first, followed by the Beloved Disciple, where both saw the wrappings. The Beloved Disciple believed immediately. He was the first full believer. They then both went home (20:3–10).

In the second scene, Mary Magdalene returned to the tomb, to be addressed by two Angels. She turned to see Jesus, but did not yet recognise him, mistaking him for the gardener. She asked where the body had been laid. Jesus spoke to her by name. She immediately believed, and obeyed his order to go to tell the disciples. Being called by name had brought her to faith. She was no longer in darkness as she had been earlier (20:11–18).

The first scene of the second act took place on the evening of that same day, in a locked room where the disciples were hiding for fear of 'the Jews'; Thomas the twin was not among them. Jesus appeared, showed them his wounds and twice said, 'Peace be with you'. He breathed the Spirit upon them, and told them that he was sending them as his father had sent him, with power to forgive sin (20:19–23).

In the second scene Thomas joined the others, to be told that they had seen the Lord. He refused to believe unless he saw and touched the wounds of Jesus (20:24–25).

The next scene took place a week later, when Thomas had joined them. Jesus again appeared, and invited Thomas to touch his wounds. Thomas, the archetypical realist, did not need to touch. He saw, and immediately believed, addressing Jesus as his Lord and his God. John has Thomas repeat his statement in the prologue to the gospel, that the Word was God.

Unlike the Beloved Disciple Thomas had believed because of what he had seen, but Jesus then said that all who believe without seeing him would be blessed (20:26–29).

The first edition of the Gospel ends with a statement of the author's purpose. It is that we may come to believe that Jesus is the Messiah, the Son of God, and that through him we might have life in his name (20:30–31). A constant theme of the Gospel has been to present us with a stark choice, between the darkness of disbelief, bringing death, and the light of faith, bringing life in the Spirit.

Epilogue (Chapter 21)

As time went by the community to which the Gospel had been addressed encountered a number of problems, which are addressed in this later epilogue. One was the question of authority. Another was the death of the Beloved Disciple, about whom a misunderstanding had arisen that Jesus had said that he would not die.

With a number of the other disciples, Peter had returned to his trade as a fisherman in Galilee. After a fruitless night Jesus appeared, standing on the beach. They did not recognise him immediately. At his command they cast the net, to take a miraculous catch of fish. The first to recognise Jesus was the Beloved Disciple. Peter then swam ashore. The rest followed, where Jesus invited them to eat a breakfast of fish that he had prepared for them. It was Peter who hauled in the fish that they had caught. We recall that the Beloved Disciple had stood back to allow Peter to enter the tomb first.

Peter was now being depicted as the leader. But what of his earlier denials? He had then denied Jesus three times. He was now brought to express his love to Jesus three times. The metaphor of his leadership was changed from fisherman to shepherd. He was told that, like Jesus, he would lay down his life for his sheep (21:1–19).

Asked by Peter about the Beloved Disciple, Jesus had said, 'If it is my will that he remain until I come what is that to you? Follow me!' This response had occasioned the misunderstanding, as the gospel explains (21:20–23).

The Gospel finally ends with the claim that it is based on the true testimony of the Beloved Disciple, who remains the model of faith and discipleship for the community. In the final verse John accurately tells us that his Gospel does not merely attempt to set out a historically accurate account of all that Jesus said and did (20:24–25).

- *What three important things does John tell us about Jesus in his Gospel?*

Further Reading

Reading the whole of the New Testament with the aid of this small book by a retired lawyer who makes no claim to be a scholar has at least, I hope, whetted your appetite for deeper and sounder insights by real experts.

It is not my intention to finish with any attempt at a detailed bibliography. There are a small number of readily available works, however, that will handsomely repay study, and I recommend them.

They are all written in a style suitable for interested lay readers who do not have the scholarly tools expected of professionals.

First there is the following work by Francis Moloney sdb, an Australian scholar who has held major academic positions in several universities, most recently as Professor of New Testament at the Catholic University of America. He discusses all four gospels, and illustrates a method of deeper reading in respect of a short passage in each. I have relied extensively on this work in writing the chapters on the gospels.

The living voice of the Gospel: the Gospels today (2006)

In his recently (2015) published *Reading the New Testament in the Church: a primer for pastors, religious educators and believers*, Moloney deals succintly with the theology of the New Testament.

Next, there is a series of paperback works on all four gospels by another eminent Australian scripture scholar, Brendan Byrne sj, Professor of New Testament at Jesuit Theological College, Parkville, Victoria. They each contain an extensive bibliography for those interested in further study.

A costly freedom: a theological reading of Mark's gospel (2008)
Lifting the burden: reading Matthew's gospel in the church today (2004)
The hospitality of God: a reading of Luke's gospel (2000)
Life Abounding: a reading of John's gospel (2014)

For an introductory overview of St Paul and his letters

A friendly guide to Paul (2014), Christopher J Monaghan

All of the above are available from www.garrattpublishing.com.au

For a more detailed study

An introduction to the study of Paul 3rd ed (2015) David G Horrell
www.fishpond.com.au

For a more detailed and scholarly overview of the whole New Testament, with comprehensive theological insights

An introduction to the New Testament: an introduction 3rd ed (2012), Pheme Perkins
Available in paper or as ebook
www.paulistpress.com

Image credits

Cover   www.immanuelstreatham.org.uk/ChristPantokrator2.htm
Fig 1.1   www.biblesnet.com/maps3/Palestine in Jesus Times.jpg
Fig 1.2   James Emery Galilee landscape_0873 www.flickr.com/photos/62126383@N00/507797526
Fig 1.3   Morrissey et al *Out of the desert* Bk 1, 1997, p. 46
Fig 1.4   Morrissey et al *Out of the desert* Bk 2, 1998, p.181
Fig 2.1   Janet Morrissey
Fig 2.2   Codex Vaticanus: Image used by permission from the Center for the Study of New Testament Manuscripts (www.csntm.org).
Fig 2.3   Codex Sinaiticus: Image used by permission from the Center for the Study of New Testament Manuscripts (www.csntm.org).
Fig. 2.4   Codex Alexandrinus:Image used by permission from the Center for the Study of New Testament Manuscripts (www.csntm.org).
Fig 2.5   Codex Bezae: Copyright © Cambridge University Library. Licensed under a Creative Commons Attribution-NonCommercial 3.0 Unported License (CC BY-NC 3.0)
Fig 2.6   commons.wikimedia.org/wiki/File:Qumran.jpeg
Fig 4.1   Morrissey et al *Living Religion* 2nd ed, 1993, p. 88
Fig 6.1   http://biblescripture.net/Philippi.jpeg
Fig 9.1   By Ploync (Own work) [CC BY 3.0] commons.wikimedia.org/wiki/File%3AAncient_Corinth_3.jpg

Fig 14.1	By Scriptorium of the Lorsch Abbey (Hofschule Karls des Großen), Germany [Public domain], via Wikimedia Commons commons.wikimedia.org/wiki/File:Codexaureus_19.jpg
Fig 14.2	Alan Hogan & Janet Morrissey
Fig 15.1	commons.wikimedia.org/wiki/File%3ACodexaureus_21.jpg
Fig 17.1	http://oneyearbibleimages.com/colossae.jpg
Fig 19.1	commons.wikimedia.org/wiki/File:Codexaureus_17.jpg
Fig 23.1	commons.wikimedia.org/wiki/File:Codexaureus_23.jpg
Fig 24.1	commons.wikimedia.org/wiki/File:Duccio_di_Buoninsegna_-_Pentecost_-_WGA06739.jpg
Fig. 26.1	biblescripture.net/SevenChurches.jpeg
Fig 29.1	commons.wikimedia.org/wiki/File:Codexaureus_25.jpg

Index

Acts: viii, xviii, 5, 9, 17, 21, 31–35, 41, 42, 45, 46, 47, 48, 50, 51, 52, 55, 56, 57, 65, 72, 76, 84, 97, 103, 123, 128, 129, 130, 131, 133, 134, 136, 137, 153, 154, 155, 159, 161, 165, 166, 168, 169, 173, 180.
    authorship, 31, 32, 33, 35, 41, 46, 51, 52, 55, 65, 76, 84, 153, 154, 155, 159, 161, 165, 166, 173.
Apocalypse: 177, 178
    apocalyptic writing, 177
Apollos: 56, 61, 72, 130, 169.
Aquila: 56, 57, 60, 65, 66, 72, 130, 134, 168, 169.
Barnabas: 33, 34, 41, 45, 46, 47, 76, 103, 115, 127, 153, 162, 163, 164, 165, 166.
Canon
    evolution of, 25, 26, 27
    meaning, 25.
Colossae: 93, 94.
Corinth: 34, 39, 42, 48, 55, 56, 57, 61, 62, 65, 69, 76, 128, 130, 168, 169.
Council of Jerusalem: 41, 153, 159, 163, 166.
Ephesus: 34, 48, 51, 56, 57, 61, 62, 93, 94, 97, 128, 130, 131, 132, 134, 169, 178, 180, 185.
Galatia: 34, 38, 45, 47, 48, 75, 169.
Gospel
    how to read, xii, xvii, 13, 26.
    synoptic, 79, 192, 206.
    criticism, types of, 81.
Herod the Great: 4, 5.

Herod Agrippa: 5, 32, 171.
Herod Antipas: 5.
Holy Land, see Palestine
James: 5, 46, 47, 75, 87, 103, 107, 109, 123, 125, 149, 155, 163, 165, 173.
Johannine literature: 173
    authorship, 183, 184.
    Gospel of, 26, 79, 85, 183
    letters, 75, 187–189.
John, 107, 108, 117, 123, 141, 155, 157, 158, 161, 163, 178, 179.
John th Baptist, 5, 10, 86, 87, 106, 108, 109, 138, 139, 164, 192, 193, 196, 197, 198.
Jewish people: 7, 8, 46, 52, 85, 104, 116, 141, 148, 149, 160, 164, 184, 196, 198.
    Essenes, 10.
    Pharisees, 9, 10, 104, 107, 108, 110, 140, 144, 199, 200,
    priests and levites, 4, 8, 9, 10, 85, 110, 118, 120, 199, 201,
    Sadducees, 9.
    Samaritans, 10, 11, 193, 197,
    Scribes, 10, 88, 104, 107, 108, 110, 140, 144, 145, 146.
    Zealots, 10.
Judas: 5, 41, 46, 47, 76, 88, 111, 146, 147, 155, 173, 194, 199, 200, 202, 203.
Judea: 33, 56, 66, 109, 153, 157, 160.
Jude: 75, 173, 174, 175, 176.
Luke: xviii, 13, 17, 26, 31, 32, 33, 35, 41, 46, 51, 52, 55, 58, 65, 76, 78, 79, 80, 84, 97, 135, 136–151, 153–171, 194.
Mark: xii, 8, 13, 26, 47, 76, 78, 79, 80, 83–89, 102, 103, 104, 109, 123, 137, 142, 144, 145, 146.
Matthew: xii, xvii, xviii, 13, 21, 26, 47, 78, 79, 80, 84, 101–113, 124, 137, 140, 145, 146, 147, 148, 150, 173, 175, 194.
Melchizedek: 117, 119, 120.
New Testament Documents: viii, 3, 18, 23, 42, 75,
    Codex Alexandrinus, 18, 211.
    Codex Bezae, 18,
    Codex Sinaiticus, 18, 20, 211.
    Codex Vaticanus, 18, 19, 211.
    cursive script, 18, 22.

uncial script, 18, 19, 22.
Vulgate, 22,
writing materials, 17, 23.
Onesimus: 94, 97.
Palestine:: 3, 5, 103, 154, 162, 173
    geography, 170
    history, 6, 10,
    language, 13,
    politics, 5, 6, 10,
    Nazareth, 7, 11, 12, 13, 15, 86, 106, 107, 108, 139, 140, 147, 204.
Paul
    Antioch, at, 34, 41, 45, 46, 47, 48, 56, 76, 103, 136, 153, 163, 164, 165, 166, 169.
    Athens, in, 42, 55, 56, 57, 61, 128, 168,
    first missionary journey, 33, 45, 165
    journey to Rome, 33, 129,
    second missionary journey, 42, 55, 76, 127.
    Letters
        authentic, xvii, 37, 38, 71, 72, 92.
        Deutero Pauline, 37, 91–92.
        how to read, 38–40
        parts, 52, 67, 71,
        pseudonymous, 38, 91, 92,
        pastoral, 38, 43, 76, 127, 128,
    trial before Felix, 34, 170, 171
    women, attitude to, 38, 58, 59, 71–73, 129, 132.
Peter: xviii, xx, 5, 8, 13, 17, 26, 32, 33, 45, 46, 47, 57, 65, 75, 76, 84, 87, 88, 89, 102, 103, 107, 108, 109, 110, 141, 142, 143, 146, 147, 149, 153, 155, 157, 158, 161, 162, 163, 165, 167, 173, 175, 183, 194, 195, 198, 202, 204, 206, 208.
Philemon: 37, 51, 53, 54, 94.
Philippi: 5, 42, 52, 128, 167.
Priscilla: 56, 57, 61, 65, 66, 72, 130, 168, 169,.
Revelation, see Apocalypse
Rome
    Christians in, 39, 56, 65, 66, 75, 104, 116, 179.
Sadducees: 9, 10, 108, 110, 145.

Scriptures: vii, xi, xiii, xx, 3, 11, 13, 14, 15, 16, 18, 22, 26, 42, 68, 85, 91, 102, 103, 116, 117, 119, 121, 124, 125, 136, 140, 146, 150, 161, 175, 178, 198.
Silas: 34, 41, 42, 46, 47, 48, 55, 76, 166, 167, 168, 169.
Simeon Niger: 46.
Silvanus, see Silas
Synoptics: 79–81.
Thessalonica: 167–168.
Timothy: 21, 38, 39, 42, 43, 48, 50, 52, 53, 55, 57, 62, 92, 97, 115, 116, 127, 128, 131, 133, 134, 166, 167, 168, 169.
Titus: 6, 38, 62, 127, 128, 129, 131, 132.

Lightning Source UK Ltd.
Milton Keynes UK
UKOW01f0443070218
317473UK00002B/179/P